P9-CDS-799

True Devotion to Mary

True Devotion to Mary

St. Louis-Marie Grignion de Montfort

Translated by Mark L. Jacobson

Aventine Press

Copyright © February 2007 by Mark L. Jacobson

Cover image: The Annunciation: Gabriel Announces Christ's Birth to Mary, from an illuminated manuscript entitled "Hours of the Virgin", courtesy of the National Library of the Netherlands, The Hague, The Netherlands.

Without limiting the rights under copyright reserved above, no part of this publication may be reproduced, stored in or introduced into a retrieval system, or transmitted, in any form or by any means (electronic, mechanical, photocopying, recording, or otherwise), without the prior written permission of both the copyright owner and the publisher of this book.

Published by Aventine Press
1023 4th Ave #204
San Diego CA, 92101
www.aventinepress.com

ISBN: 1-59330-470-6

Printed in the United States of America

ALL RIGHTS RESERVED

Dedicated to
my wife and
our two daughters,
to my mother and
my mother-in-law,
and to Mary,
Mother of the Redeemed.

Table of Contents

Introduction

All to Jesus, I surrender;
All to Him I freely give.
I will ever love and trust Him,
In His presence daily live.
I surrender all, I surrender all,
All to Thee, my blessed Savior,
I surrender all.

(From the hymn "I Surrender All",
by Jueson W. Van DeVenter, 1896)

Composed nearly two centuries after "True Devotion to Mary" was written, the words of this Protestant hymn provide a fitting summary of St. Louis-Marie's decidedly Roman Catholic approach to devotion, holiness and spirituality. In "True Devotion", he invites each of us to surrender, in love and in trust, all that we are and all that we have to our blessed Savior. In freely offering ourselves to Him, we renew our baptismal promises, and consecrate ourselves to live each day in His presence as His devoted servants.

But if St. Louis-Marie is truly calling us to surrender all to Jesus Christ, why does he focus so much on Mary, His Mother? As this book so beautifully and convincingly explains, it is because Mary, the faithful handmaid of the Lord, who is "ever humble and in conformity with His will", is a Mother worthy of our trust and devotion, on whom we can depend to keep, protect and make exceedingly fruitful all that we entrust to her, for the salvation of souls and for the greater glory of God. As St. Louis-Marie explains, "If therefore we firmly establish this devotion to the Most Holy Virgin, it is only to more perfectly establish devotion to Jesus Christ, it is only to provide an easy and assured way to find Him." And this way of Mary is not without Divine precedent. By going to Jesus through Mary, we are taking the same humble way to Our Lord as He first took in coming to us. This is the essence of "True Devotion to Mary".

By far the most well-known of the writings of St. Louis-Marie Grignion de Montfort, this treatise was called "True Devotion to Mary" (or something similar) almost from its first publication, although the original manuscript was untitled. This new translation maintains that longstanding tradition. In addition to being untitled, the original manuscript had no chapter headings. The chapter divisions and headings in this translation are new; their purpose is to provide a broad outline of the work, while allowing the original text to speak for itself. An appendix of prayers, not part of the original manuscript, has been added as a reference for the reader.

The translation into English was done with the goal of remaining faithful to the structure of the original French, preserving the phraseology, sentence composition and word flow as much as possible. This rather literal style was employed in order to provide the English-speaking reader with some experience of the beauty and style of the original French text. Latin phrases have been left intact and italicized; bracketed translations are provided where the meaning is not clear from the surrounding text. Other notes, also enclosed in brackets, have been kept to an absolute minimum.

In reading and meditating on this inspired work of Marian piety and devotion, one quickly gets the impression that it proceeded from the heart of a truly holy soul. St. Louis-Marie Grignion de Montfort was indeed a true saint in every sense of the word. Born in 1673, he was from an early age a deeply spiritual person with a burning passion for the salvation of souls. Hearing the call to the priesthood during his college years, he eventually set out for Paris in the year 1693 to study in the seminary of St. Sulpice.

He chose to make the long journey on foot, after refusing out of humility to accept the horse offered to him by his family. While making his way through the French countryside, he exchanged his new coat for the rags of a beggar, gave away all of his money, and resolved from then on to rely only on God's Providence and the mercy of others. He devoted himself to his studies for the next 7 years, and was ordained to the priesthood in Paris in June 1700. St. Louis the priest spent the remaining 16 years of his life caring for the poor, preaching missions, and leading people to holiness through devotion and consecration to the Holy Virgin. His was a life of joyous penance, heroic sacrifice, and patient perseverance in the face of setbacks, misunderstandings, and opposition even from within the Church. The many inspired writings he authored, the religious orders he founded, and the lasting effects of his preaching all attest to the holiness of this humble Apostle of Mary. Pope John Paul II once said that "the reading of this book marked a decisive turning point in my life", and of the author he said "St. Louis-Marie is for me a figure of reference who has enlightened me in my most decisive moments". Beatified in 1888, and canonized in 1947, St. Louis-Marie continues to inspire the Church on Earth, even as he intercedes for us from his glorious home in Heaven. His feast day is celebrated by the universal Church on April 28.

In re-offering this work to the public, my prayer is that St. Louis-Marie Grignion de Montfort will inspire a new and receptive group of readers to become faithful servants of the Most Holy Virgin Mary by embracing this True Devotion. I pray with St. Louis-Marie that a great army of loyal soldiers may be raised up to do battle against evil under the direction and guidance of the Immaculate Queen of Heaven. Then, and only then, will Jesus Christ reign triumphant in the hearts of His faithful ones.

Glory to Jesus in Mary!

Chapter 1

The Glories of Mary

It was through the Most Holy Virgin Mary that Jesus Christ came into the world, and it is through her that He must reign in the world.

Mary was most hidden during her life, which is why she is called by the Holy Spirit and by the Church *Alma Mater*: Mother hidden and secret. Her humility was so profound that while on Earth she had no more powerful and enduring attraction than to hide herself from herself and from every other creature, to be known by God alone.

In order to fulfill the requests she made of Him that He hide, impoverish, and humble her, God took pleasure in concealing her from the view of almost every human creature at her conception, at her birth, during her life, in her mysteries, at her resurrection and at her assumption. Even her parents did not really know her; and the angels often asked of each other: *Quae est ista?:* Who is she? Because the Most High had hidden her from them; or, if there was something He revealed to them about her, there was infinitely more that He concealed from them.

God the Father agreed that she would work no miracles during her life, or at least none that drew attention, even though He had given her the power to do so. God the Son agreed that she would speak but rarely, even though He had communicated to her His Wisdom. God the Holy Spirit consented that His Apostles and Evangelists would speak but little of her and only as much as was necessary to make known Jesus Christ, even though she was His faithful Spouse.

Mary is the excellent masterpiece of the Most High, the knowledge and possession of whom He reserves for Himself. Mary is the admirable Mother of the Son, whom He took pleasure in humbling and concealing during her life, in deference to her humility, addressing her with the name woman: *mulier*, as if she were a stranger, even though in His heart He esteemed her and loved her more than all the angels and men. Mary is the sealed fountain, and the faithful Spouse of the Holy Spirit, wherein only He may enter; Mary is the sanctuary and resting place of the Holy Trinity, where God is found more magnificently and divinely than in any other place in the universe, except in His abode above the cherubim and seraphim; and no other creature no matter how pure is permitted to enter there without great privilege.

I say with the saints: the divine Mary is the earthly Paradise of the New Adam, wherein He became incarnate by the working of the Holy Spirit, to work there His incomprehensible marvels. She is the great and divine world of God, where there are beautiful things and ineffable treasures. She is the magnificence of the Most High, where He has hidden, as in His bosom, His unique Son, and in Him everything that is most excellent and most precious. Oh! oh! what great and secret things this powerful God has worked in this wonderful creature, as she herself was obliged to say, despite her profound humility: *Fecit mihi magna qui potens est*: The world does not know this, because it is incapable and unworthy of it.

The saints have said wonderful things about this Holy City of God; and never were they more eloquent nor more content, as they themselves have acknowledged, as when they spoke of her. They exclaim further that the greatness of her merits, which she has raised up even to the Throne of the Divinity, cannot be fully known; that the breadth of her charity, which she has spread out beyond the farthest reaches of the Earth, cannot be measured; that the greatness of her power, which she holds even over a God, cannot be comprehended; and finally, that the depths of her humility and of all her virtues and graces, which are an abyss, cannot be fathomed. Oh incomprehensible heights! Oh ineffable breadth! Oh immeasurable greatness! Oh impenetrable depths!

Every day, from one end of the Earth to the other, from the highest heavens to the deepest depths, everything preaches, everything proclaims the wonders of Mary. The nine choirs of angels, men of every sex, age, condition of life, religion, the good and the bad, even the demons are obliged to call her blessed, whether they want to or not, by the sheer force of the truth. All the angels in Heaven cry out to her unceasingly: *Sancta, sancta, sancta Maria, Dei Genitrix et Virgo* [Holy, Holy, Holy Mary, God-Bearer and Virgin]; and offer her millions upon millions of times day in and day out the angelic salutation: *Ave, Maria* [Hail Mary], prostrating themselves before her, and imploring her to honor them with just one of her commands. Even St. Michael, says St. Augustine, despite being the Prince of the entire celestial court, is the most zealous in bestowing upon her, and causing others to give to her, all sorts of honors, always awaiting the privilege to be sent forth by her word to give aid to one of her servants.

All the Earth is full of her glory, especially among the Christians, where she is regarded as guardian and protector in many kingdoms, provinces, dioceses and towns. So many cathedrals are consecrated to God in her name. There is not one church without an altar in her honor: not one country or district without a miraculous image of her, where all kinds of diseases are cured and every kind of good is obtained. So many confraternities and congregations in her honor! So many religious orders under her name and protection! So many men and women in all the confraternities, so many men and women religious from every religious order who proclaim her praises and announce her mercies! There is not one small child who does not praise her in saying the *Ave Maria*; there are hardly any sinners who, even in their hardness of heart, do not have some spark of hope in her; there is not even one demon in Hell who, in fearing her, does not respect her.

In light of all of this, one must say in truth with the saints: *De Maria nunquam satis*: Mary has not yet been praised, exalted, loved or served nearly enough; she is still deserving of more praise, honor, love and service.

Furthermore, in light of all of this, one must say with the Holy Spirit: *Omnis gloria ejus filiæ Regis ab intus*: All the glory of the King's daughter is within: as if all her exterior glory, which makes all of Heaven and Earth envious, were nothing in comparison to that interior glory which she has received from the Creator, and which is unknowable by mere creatures who are incapable of penetrating the secret of the secrets of the King.

And finally, in light of all of this, one must exclaim with the Apostle: *Nec oculus vidit, nec auris audivit, nec in cor hominus ascendit*: Eye has not seen, nor ear has heard, nor heart has understood the beauties, the greatness, the excellence of Mary, the miracle of miracles of grace, nature and glory. If you desire to comprehend Mary, says one saint, comprehend the Son. She is a worthy Mother of God; *Hic taceat omnis lingua*: Let every tongue rest in silence.

Chapter 2

The Necessity of Mary

It is truly my heart which has dictated that which I have just written, and with singular joy, in order to show that the divine Mary has been largely unknown until now, and this is one of the reasons that Jesus Christ is not yet known as He should be. Certainly therefore, if the knowledge of and the reign of Jesus Christ are to come about in the world, they will come about as necessary consequences of the knowledge of and the reign of the Most Holy Virgin Mary, who brought Him into the world the first time, and will bring about His dazzling return.

I admit with the entire Church that Mary, being but a mere creature formed by the hand of the Most High, when compared to His infinite Majesty, is less than an atom, or more precisely is nothing at all, because only He is the "I Am Who Am", and by consequence, this great Lord, who is forever independent and self-sufficient, did not have and does not now have any absolute need of the Most Holy Virgin in order to accomplish His will and manifest His glory. His will is wholly sufficient to accomplish anything.

I say, however, taking all things into consideration, that since God desired to begin and bring to completion His greatest works by means of the Most Holy Virgin from the very moment He formed her, one must believe that He, being God, has never changed His ways throughout all the centuries, and will never change His manner of thinking nor His manner of acting.

God the Father did not give His Unique Son to the world except through Mary; for four thousand years, no matter how much the patriarchs expressed their longings, no matter how much the prophets and saints of the old covenant asked to possess this treasure, no one but Mary merited Him and found grace before God by the power of her prayers and the loftiness of her virtues. Since the world was unworthy, says St. Augustine, to receive the Son of God directly from the Father's hands, He gave Him to Mary in order that the world might receive Him through her.

God the Holy Spirit formed Jesus Christ in Mary, but only after having asked her consent by means of one of the highest ministers in His court.

God the Father communicated His fecundity to Mary as far as a pure creature is capable of it, in order to give Her the power to produce His Son and all the members of His Mystical Body.

God the Son descended into her virginal womb, like the New Adam into His earthly Paradise, to take pleasure in being there and to bring about in secret His marvels of grace. This God-made-man found His freedom by imprisoning Himself in her womb; He showed forth His might by letting Himself be carried by this young girl; He found His glory and that of His Father by hiding His splendors from all creatures here below, to reveal them to no one but Mary; He glorified His independence and His majesty by being dependent on this lovable Virgin at His conception, His birth, His presentation in the Temple, His hidden life of thirty years, even at His death, where her presence was necessary in order for Him to offer one sacrifice together with her, and to be immolated by her consent to the Father, just as before when Isaac was offered by Abraham's consent to the will of God. It was she who nursed, fed, cared for, raised and sacrificed Him for us.

O admirable and incomprehensible dependence of a God, about which the Holy Spirit could not remain silent in the Gospel, even though He concealed almost all of the wonderful things that this Incarnate Wisdom did in His hidden life, in order to show us the infinite worth and infinite glory of it. Jesus Christ gave more glory to God His Father by the submission He had toward His Mother during those thirty years, than He would have in converting the entire world by performing the greatest of marvels. Oh! how mightily is God glorified when one places oneself in submission to Mary in order to please Him, following the example of Jesus Christ, our unique model!

If we closely examine the rest of the life of Jesus Christ, we will see that He desired to begin His miracles through Mary. He sanctified St. John in the womb of his mother St. Elizabeth through the words of Mary; as soon as she spoke, John was sanctified, and this was His first and greatest miracle of grace. At the wedding of Cana, He changed water to wine as a result of her humble prayer, and this was His first miracle of nature. He started and continued His miracles through Mary; and He will continue them through Mary until the end of time.

God the Holy Spirit, being sterile within the Godhead, that is to say not producing any other divine Person, became fruitful through Mary, whom He took as His Spouse. It is with her, and in her, and from her that He produced His greatest Masterpiece, which is a God-made-man, and that He produces, every day until the end of the world, the predestined members of the Body of this Head so worthy of adoration; this is why the more He finds Mary, His cherished and inseparable Spouse, in a soul, the more efficacious and powerful He becomes in producing Jesus Christ in that soul and that soul in Jesus Christ.

It is not that one would say that the Most Holy Virgin gives fecundity to the Holy Spirit, as if He did not possess it Himself, since, being God, He has the fecundity or the capacity to produce like the Father and the Son, though He does not exercise it, not producing any other divine Person. But one would say that the Holy Spirit, by means of the Holy Virgin, through whom He desires to work, although He has no absolute need to, exercised His fecundity in producing Jesus Christ and His members in her and through her; a mystery of grace unknown even among the wisest and most spiritual of Christians.

The manner in which the three Persons of the Most Holy Trinity acted in accomplishing the Incarnation and the first coming of Jesus Christ, is continued by them every day in an invisible manner in the Church, and will be continued until the end of the ages at the final return of Jesus Christ.

God the Father made an assemblage of all the waters, which He called the ocean; He made an assemblage of all graces, which He called Mary. Our great God has a treasure, or very rich storehouse in which He concealed all that He has that is beautiful, magnificent, rare and precious, even unto His own Son; and this vast treasure is none other than Mary, whom the saints have called the Treasure of the Lord, whose abundance enriches all mankind.

God the Son communicated to His Mother everything He acquired by His life and His death, His infinite merits and excellent virtues, and He made her the treasury of everything His Father gave Him as an inheritance; it is through her that He applies His merits to the members of His Body; she is His mysterious channel, she is His aqueduct through which His mercies gently and abundantly flow.

God the Holy Spirit communicated His ineffable gifts to Mary, His faithful Spouse; and He chose her to be the dispenser of everything He possesses in such a way that she distributes all of

His gifts and His graces to whomever she wishes, as much as she wishes, in the manner she wishes, and whenever she wishes, and He does not give any Heavenly gift to men which does not pass through her virginal hands. Because such is the will of God, who willed that we receive everything through Mary; because in this way God will adorn, elevate and honor she who impoverished, humbled and hid herself even unto nothingness by her profound humility throughout her entire life. These are the sentiments of the Church and the Holy Fathers.

If I were speaking to the intellectuals of our time, I would prove at length everything I am now simply stating, using Sacred Scripture and the Holy Fathers from which I would recount passages in Latin, and to which I would add many solid arguments such as those found in the lengthy deductions by R.P. Poiré in his "Triple Crown of the Holy Virgin". But because I am speaking particularly to the poor and the simple, who being of good will and having greater faith than the typical intellectual, believe more simply and more meritoriously, I am content with simply stating the Truth, without stopping to cite to them all the Latin passages, which they do not understand, although I do not neglect to quote a few without a great deal of explanation. Let us continue.

Since grace perfects nature and glory perfects grace, it is certain that in Heaven our Lord is still as much the Son of Mary as He was on Earth, and as a consequence, He has maintained the submission and the obedience of the most perfect of all children with regard to the greatest of all mothers. But one must guard against finding in this dependence some inferiority or imperfection in Jesus Christ. Because Mary, being infinitely beneath her Son who is God, does not command Him as a mother here below would command her child who is beneath her. Mary, being totally transformed in God by the grace and glory which transforms all the saints in Him, does not ask, desire or do anything that is contrary to the eternal and unchangeable will of God. Thus when one reads in the writings of St. Bernard, St. Bernardine, St. Bonaventure, and others, that in Heaven and on Earth everything, even God Himself, is subject to the Holy Virgin, they mean to say that the authority that God consented to give to her is so great that it appears that she has the same power as God, and that her prayers and requests are so powerful before God that they are always taken as commands by His Majesty, who never resists the prayers of His dear Mother, because she is ever humble and in conformity with His will.

If Moses, by the force of his prayer, halted the anger of God toward the Israelites in such a powerful way that this most high and infinitely merciful Lord, unable to resist him, asked Moses the permission to become angry and punish this rebellious people, then what are we to think, with all the more reason, about the prayer of the humble Mary, the most worthy Mother of God, which is more powerful before His Majesty than the prayers and intercessions of all the angels and saints in Heaven and on Earth?

Mary commands the angels and the saints in Heaven. As recompense for her profound humility, God gave her the power and the commission to fill with saints the empty thrones from which the apostate angels fell because of their pride. Such is the will of the Most High, who exalts the humble, that the Heavens, the Earth and Hell, whether they want to or not, should yield to the commands of the humble Mary, whom He made the Queen of Heaven and Earth, the commander of His armies, the Treasury of His treasures, the dispenser of His graces, the worker of His great wonders, the restorer of the human race, the mediatrix of men, the exterminator of the enemies of God, and His faithful partner in His grandeurs and in His triumphs.

God the Father desires to make children through Mary until the end of the world, and He says these words to her: *In Jacob inhabita*: remain in Jacob, which is to say make your abode and your residence in my predestined children, prefigured by Jacob, and never in the children of the Devil nor the damned, prefigured by Esau [see Chapter 7].

As in natural and bodily generation there is a father and a mother, so also in supernatural and spiritual generation there is a Father, who is God, and a Mother, who is Mary. All the true children of God and the predestined have God as Father and Mary as Mother; and whoever does not have Mary as his Mother does not have God as his Father. This is why the damned, such as the heretics, schismatics, and others, who hate or regard with contempt or indifference the Most Holy Virgin, do not have God as their father, even though they boast that they do, because they do not have Mary as their Mother; since, if they had her as their Mother, they would love her and honor her as a true and good child naturally loves and honors his mother who gave him life.

The most infallible and indisputable sign for distinguishing a heretic, a man of bad doctrine, a damned from a predestined is that the heretics and the damned have nothing but disdain or indifference toward the Most Holy Virgin, trying by their words and examples, overtly or in secret, sometimes under good pretense, to diminish her cult and the love that is shown for her. Alas! God the Father did not tell Mary to make her abode in them, because they are Esaus [see Chapter 7].

God the Son wants to form Himself and, so to speak, to incarnate Himself every day in His members, by means of His dear Mother, and He says to her: *In Israel hereditare*: Take Israel as your inheritance. It is as if He had said: God the Father gave me as an inheritance all the nations of the Earth, all men good and bad, the predestined and the damned; I will lead some by the rod of gold, and the others by the rod of iron; I will be the father and the advocate of some, the just avenger of others, and the judge of all; but for you, my dear Mother, you will have as your inheritance and possession only the predestined, who were prefigured by Israel; as their good Mother, you will give birth to them, nourish them, raise them; as their queen, you will guide them, govern them and defend them.

A man and a man is born of her, says the Holy Spirit: *Homo et homo natus est in ea.* According to the explanation of several Church Fathers, the first man who is born of Mary is the God-Man, Jesus Christ; the second is purely human, a child of God and of Mary by adoption. If Jesus Christ, the head of Man, is born from her, then the predestined, who are members of the head, must also be born of her as a necessary consequence. The same mother does not bring into the world the head without the members, nor the members without the head; otherwise this would be a monster of nature; in the same way, in the order of grace, the head and the members are born of the same Mother; and if a member of the Mystical Body of Jesus Christ, that is to say a predestined, were to be born of a mother other than Mary, who produced the head, this would be neither a predestined, nor a member of Jesus Christ, but a monster in the order of grace.

In addition, since Jesus is at present as much as ever the fruit of Mary, as Heaven and Earth repeat to her thousands upon thousands of times every day: "And blessed is the fruit of your womb, Jesus", it is certain that Jesus Christ is as much the fruit and the work of Mary for each individual who possesses Him as for the whole world in general; in such a way that if a certain member of the faithful has Jesus Christ formed in his heart, he can boldly say, "Thanks be to Mary, for that which I possess is her effect and her fruit, and without her I would not have Him";

and these words that St. Paul applied to himself are even more rightfully applied to her: *Quos iterum parturio, donec in vobis formetur Christus*: I give birth daily to God's children, until Jesus Christ my Son is formed in them in the fullness of His age. St. Augustine, surpassing himself and everything I have just said, says that all the predestined, in order to be in conformity with the image of the Son of God, are in this world concealed in the womb of the Most Holy Virgin where they are kept, nourished, maintained and raised by this good Mother, until she begets them into glory after death, which is precisely the day of their birth, as the Church calls the death of the righteous. Oh mystery of grace unknown among the damned and little known among the predestined!

God the Holy Spirit desires to form the elect in her and through her, and He says to her, *In electis meis mitte radices*: Implant, my beloved and my Spouse, the roots of all your virtues in my elect, so that they might grow from virtue to virtue and from grace to grace. I took so much pleasure in you when you lived on Earth in the practice of the most sublime virtues, that I desire to find you again on Earth, without your ceasing to be in Heaven. To this end, reproduce yourself in my elect: that I might take pleasure in seeing in them the roots of your invincible faith, your profound humility, your universal mortification, your sublime prayers, your ardent charity, your unwavering hope, and all your virtues. You are forever my Spouse, as faithful, as pure and as fruitful as ever: may your faith produce for Me the faithful; may your purity produce for Me virgins, may your fecundity produce for Me the elect, My temples.

When Mary has implanted her roots in a soul, she produces there such marvels of grace as only she can produce because she is the only fruitful Virgin who was and forever will be unequaled in purity and fecundity.

Mary produced, together with the Holy Spirit, the greatest thing which ever was and ever will be, that is a God-Man, and she will consequently produce the greatest things during the end times. The formation and education of the greatest saints who will be inhabit the world at its end is reserved for her, because she alone is that singular and miraculous Virgin who can produce, in union with the Holy Spirit, that which is singular and extraordinary.

When the Holy Spirit, her Spouse, finds her in a soul, He flies there, He enters there fully, He communicates Himself abundantly to this soul, and in proportion to the place this soul has given to His Spouse; and one of the primary reasons the Holy Spirit does not perform magnificent marvels in souls these days is that He does not find in them a sufficient union with His faithful and inseparable Spouse. I say inseparable Spouse, because from the moment this substantial Love of the Father and the Son espoused Mary in order to produce Jesus Christ, the head of the elect and Jesus Christ in the elect, He has never repudiated her, because she has always been faithful and fruitful.

One must evidently conclude from what I have just said:

First, that Mary received from God a great dominion over the souls of the elect; because she could not make her home in them, as God the Father directed her; she could not form them, nourish them and birth them into eternal life as their Mother, nor have them as her inheritance and her portion, nor form them in Jesus Christ and Jesus Christ in them; she could not implant in their hearts the roots of her virtues, nor be the inseparable companion of the Holy Spirit in all His works of grace; she could not, I say, do all these things if she did not have the right and the dominion over their souls by a singular grace from the Most High who, having given her power over His unique and natural Son, also gave it to her over His adopted children, not only with regard to the body, which would be but a small thing, but also with regard to the soul.

Mary is the Queen of Heaven and Earth by grace, as Jesus is their King by nature and by conquest. Just as the reign of Jesus Christ exists principally in the heart, or interior of men, according to these words: "The reign of God is within us", so also the reign of the Most Holy Virgin is principally in the interior of men, that is to say in their souls, and it is principally within these souls that she is more glorified with her Son than in all the visible creatures, and we can join with all the saints in calling her the "Queen of Hearts".

Second, one must conclude that since the Most Holy Virgin is necessary to God of a necessity which one calls hypothetical, or as a result of His will, she is all the more necessary to men in order for them to reach their final end. It is not necessary, therefore, to mix devotion to the Most Holy Virgin with devotion to the other saints, as if devotion to her were not more necessary, or were simply one option among many.

The learned and pious Suarez, of the Company of Jesus, the scholarly and devout Juste-Lipse, Doctor of Louvain, and many others, have proven irrefutably, as a consequence of the opinions of the Fathers, among others St. Augustine, St. Ephrem, deacon of Edesse, St. Cyril of Jerusalem, St. Germain of Constantinople, St. John Damascene, St. Anselm, St. Bernard, St. Bernardine, St. Thomas and St. Bonaventure, that devotion to the Most Holy Virgin is necessary for salvation, and that it is an infallible sign of damnation, which is even the opinion of Œcolampade and of other heretics, to not have esteem and love for the Holy Virgin, and that on the contrary it is an infallible sign of predestination to be completely and truly dedicated and devoted to her.

The figures and the words of the Old and New Testaments prove it, the opinions and the examples of the saints confirm it, reason and experience teach it and demonstrate it, and even the devil and his henchmen, constrained by the force of the truth, have frequently been obliged to acknowledge it in spite of themselves. Of all the passages of the Fathers and Doctors of the Church, of which I have made an ample collection for proving this truth, I will quote but one in order to be brief: *Tibi devotum esse, est arma quœdam salutis quœ Deus his dat quos vult savos fieri (S. Joan. Damas)*: "Devotion to you, O Holy Virgin", says St. John Damascene, "is an arm of salvation God gives to those He desires to save".

At this point I could recount several stories which prove the same thing, among others: that which is reported in the chronicles of St. Francis, when he saw, while in ecstasy, a great ladder that extended to Heaven, at the top of which was the Holy Virgin and by which, it was shown to him, one must ascend to attain Heaven; and that which is reported in the chronicles of St. Dominic, when 15,000 demons who were possessing the soul of a wretched heretic, near Carcassonne where St. Dominic was preaching the Rosary, were obliged in their confusion, by order of the Holy Virgin, to acknowledge many great and consoling truths regarding devotion to her with such force and clarity, that one cannot read this genuine account and the praises the devil expressed in spite of himself regarding devotion to the Most Holy Virgin, without shedding tears of joy, provided that one is indeed devoted to her.

If devotion to the Most Holy Virgin is necessary to all men simply to attain salvation, it is all the more so for those who are called to a special perfection; and I do not believe that anyone can obtain an intimate union with Our Lord and a perfect fidelity to the Holy Spirit without an intimate union with the Most Holy Virgin and a total dependence on her aid.

It is Mary alone who found favor with God, without the help
of any other mere creature. It is only through her that all who
have found favor with God since her have found it, and it is only
through her that all who are to come will find it. She was full
of grace when she was greeted by the Archangel Gabriel, she
was superabundantly filled with grace by the Holy Spirit when
He covered her with His ineffable shadow; and she has added
so greatly to this twofold fullness from day to day and from
moment to moment that she has attained a vast and inconceivable
state of grace, such that the Most High has made her the unique
Treasury of His treasures and the unique dispenser of His graces,
in order to ennoble, raise up and enrich whomever she wishes,
to permit whomever she wants to enter the narrow way to
Heaven, to permit whomever she wants, in spite of everything,
to pass through the narrow door of life, and to give the throne,
the scepter and the crown of the King to whomever she wishes.
Jesus is everywhere and always the fruit and the Son of Mary;
and Mary is everywhere the veritable tree who bears the fruit of
life, and the true Mother who produces it.

It is Mary alone to whom God gave the keys of the cellars of
divine love, and the power to enter into the most sublime and
secret ways of perfection, and to permit others therein to enter. It
is Mary alone who grants entry into the terrestrial Paradise to the
miserable children of Eve the unfaithful, there to take pleasant
walks with God, there to hide in security from their enemies,
and there to be deliciously nourished, without any more fear of
death, from the fruit of the trees of life and of the knowledge
of good and evil, and to drink deeply the heavenly waters of
this beautiful fountain which gushes abundantly there; or rather,
since she is herself this terrestrial Paradise, this virginal and
blessed land out from which the sinners Adam and Eve were
driven, she does not grant entry to anyone except those whom
she wishes to make into saints.

All the rich among the people, to use an expression of the Holy
Spirit, according to the explanation of St. Bernard, all the rich
among the people will seek your face from age to age, and
particularly at the end of the world, that is to say that the greatest
saints, the souls most rich in grace and virtue, will be the most
assiduous at praying to the Most Holy Virgin and at having
her always present as their perfect model to imitate and their
powerful aid who helps them.

I said that this would happen particularly at the end of the world,
and soon, because the Most High together with His Holy Mother
must form great saints whose holiness surpasses that of most
of the other saints, as much as the cedars of Lebanon surpass
the tiny shrubs, as was revealed to a holy soul whose life was
recorded by Mr. de Renty.

These great souls, full of grace and zeal, will be chosen to rise up
in opposition to God's enemies, who will tremble on every side;
and they will be singularly devoted to the Most Holy Virgin,
enlightened by her light, nourished by her milk, guided by her
spirit, sustained by her arms and guarded under her protection, in
such a way that they will battle with one hand and edify with the
other. With one hand, they will battle, overthrow, and crush the
heretics with their heresies, the schismatics with their schisms,
the idolaters with their idolatry, and the sinners with their
impieties; and with the other hand, they will edify the temple of
the true Solomon and the Mystical City of God, that is to say the
Most Holy Virgin, called by the Church Fathers the Temple of
Solomon and the City of God. They will draw the whole world
by their words and their examples to her true devotion, which
will attract many enemies, but also many victories and glory
for God alone. This is what was revealed to St. Vincent Ferrier,
great apostle of his century, to which he sufficiently testified in
one of his works.

This is what the Holy Spirit seems to have foretold in Psalm 58, with these words: *Et scient quia Dominus dominabitur Jacob et finium terræ; convertentur ad vesperam, et famem patientur ut canes, et circuibunt civitatem*: The Lord will reign in Jacob and throughout the whole Earth; they will be converted in the evening, and they will suffer from hunger like dogs, and they will go around the city searching for something to eat. This city to which men will be drawn at the end of the world to be converted and to satisfy their hunger for justice is the Most Holy Virgin, who is called by the Holy Spirit the City of God.

It is through Mary that the salvation of the world was begun, and it is through Mary that it must be consummated. Mary was hardly seen during the first coming of Jesus Christ, in order that men, still barely instructed and enlightened about the person of her Son, would not stray from the truth by becoming too strongly and too unthinkingly attached to her, that which apparently would have happened if she had been known, due to the admirable charms with which the Most High had endowed even her exterior; this is so true that St. Denis the Areopagite left us in writing that, when he saw her, he would have taken her for a divinity, because of her secret charms and her incomparable beauty, if the faith in which he was well confirmed had not taught him otherwise. However, at the second coming of Jesus Christ, Mary must be known and revealed by the Holy Spirit in order for her to make Jesus Christ known, loved and served, since the reasons no longer exist which had caused the Holy Spirit to conceal His Spouse during her life, and to not reveal her, except a little after the preaching of the Gospel.

God desires to reveal and show forth Mary, the masterpiece of His hands, in these end times: because she hid herself in the world and made herself less than the dust by her profound humility, having obtained from God, from His Apostles and Evangelists, that she would not be made manifest at all; and because, since she is the masterpiece of God's hands as much here below by grace as in Heaven by glory, He desires to be glorified and praised in her on Earth by the living.

Since she is the dawn that precedes and reveals the Sun of Justice, who is Jesus Christ, she should be known and seen in order that Jesus Christ be also.

Being the way by which Jesus Christ came to us the first time, she will be so also when He comes the second time, although not in the same manner.

Being the sure means and the straight and immaculate way to go to Jesus Christ and to find Him perfectly, it is through her that the holy souls who are to be resplendent in holiness must find Him. He who finds Mary finds life, that is to say Jesus Christ, who is the Way, the Truth and the Life. But one cannot find Mary if one does not look for her; and one cannot look for her if one does not know her; because one neither looks for nor desires something that is unknown. It is therefore necessary that Mary be known more than ever, to the greater knowledge and glory of the Most Holy Trinity.

Mary must shine forth more than ever in mercy, in strength and in grace in these end times: in mercy, to gather together and lovingly receive those poor sinners and all those who have strayed and who convert and return to the Catholic Church; in strength against the enemies of God, against idolaters, schismatics, heretics, Muslims and Jews, and against the hardened impious, who rebel dreadfully in order to seduce and cause to fall, by promises and by threats, anyone who is against them; and finally, she must shine forth in grace, in order to stir up and sustain the valiant soldiers and faithful servants of Jesus Christ who battle for His interests.

Finally, Mary must terrorize the devil and his henchmen like an army arrayed in battle, principally in these end times, because the devil, knowing full well that he has little time to damn souls, and much less than ever, redoubles every day his efforts and his combats; he will soon raise up cruel persecutions, and will set up terrible ambushes for the faithful servants and true children of Mary, whom he has more trouble mastering than others.

It is principally these last and cruel persecutions from the devil, which will increase every day until the reign of the Antichrist, which one must see in this first and famous prophecy and curse which God pronounced against the serpent: *Inimicitias ponam inter te et multierem, et semen tuum semen illius; ipsa conteret caput tuum, et tu insidiaberis calcaneo ejus* (Gen. 3:15): I will put enmity between you and the woman, and between her race and yours; she will crush your head, and you will wait in ambush for her heel. It is fitting here to explain this for the glory of the Most Holy Virgin, the salvation of her children, and the confusion of the devil:

God has only ever made and formed a single irreconcilable enmity, one which will endure and increase until the end: it is between Mary, His worthy Mother, and the devil, between the children and the servants of the Holy Virgin, and the children and the henchmen of Lucifer; in such a way that the one whom God has made the most terrible enemy of the devil is Mary, His Holy Mother. He even gave her, since the time of the Earthly Paradise, even though she was then only an idea in His mind, so much hatred against this cursed enemy of God, so much skill in uncovering the evil of this ancient serpent, so much power to vanquish, confound and crush this prideful blasphemer, that he dreads her, not only more than all the angels and men, but, in one sense, more than God Himself. It is not that the wrath, the hatred and the power of God are not infinitely greater than that of the Holy Virgin, since the perfections of Mary have their limits; but it is, first of all, because Satan, being proud, suffers infinitely more in being conquered by a little and humble servant of God, and her humility humiliates him more than divine power; and secondly, because God has given Mary so great a power against the demons that they have more fear, as they have often been obliged to admit in spite themselves by the mouth of the possessed, of a single sigh from her for a soul, than the prayers of all the saints, and of just one of her menaces against them than all their other torments.

That which Lucifer lost through pride, Mary gained through humility; that which Eve damned and lost through disobedience, Mary saved by obedience. Eve, in obeying the serpent, lost all of her children with her, and delivered them to him; Mary, having given herself faithfully to God, saved all her children and servants with her, and consecrated them to His Majesty.

God has put not just one enmity, but enmities, not only between Mary and the devil, but between the race of the Holy Virgin and the race of the devil; that is to say, God has put enmities, antipathies and secret hatreds between the true children and servants of the Holy Virgin and the children and slaves of the devil; they have no mutual love for each other, they have absolutely no interior connection with each other. The children of Belial, the slaves of Satan, the friends of the world (for it is the same thing), have always persecuted until today, and will persecute more than ever those who belong to the Most Holy Virgin, as long ago Cain persecuted his brother Abel, and Esau his brother Jacob, who are the types of the damned and the predestined. But the humble Mary will always have the victory over this prideful one, and so great a victory that she will even go so far as to crush his head, wherein resides his pride; she will always expose the serpent's malice; she will bring to light his infernal appearances, she will dissipate his diabolical advices, and she will protect until the end of time her faithful servants from his cruel grasp.

But the power of Mary over all the demons will radically intensify in the end times, when Satan will lie in ambush for her heel, that is to say for her humble slaves and for her poor children whom she will raise up to make war against him. They will be little and poor in the eyes of the world, and humbled before everyone like the heel, trampled and persecuted like the heel as regards the rest of the body; but in exchange, they will be rich in the grace of God, which Mary will distribute to them in abundance; great and elevated in holiness before God, superior to all creatures by their lively zeal, and so strongly supported by divine help, that with the humility of their heel, in union with Mary, they will crush the head of the devil and bring about the triumph of Jesus Christ.

Finally, God desires that His Holy Mother be known, loved and honored today more than ever before, that which will happen without doubt if the predestined enter into, with the grace and the light of the Holy Spirit, that interior and perfect practice I will bring to light in what follows. If they do so, they will see clearly, as much as faith permits, this beautiful Star of the Sea, and they will reach safe harbor, despite the tempests and pirates, in following its guidance; they will know the greatness of this Sovereign and they will consecrate themselves entirely to her service, as her subjects and slaves of love; they will experience her sweetness and her maternal goodness, and they will love her tenderly as her beloved children; they will know the mercies of which she is full, and their need where they are for her help, and they will have recourse to her in everything, as to their dear advocate and mediator with Jesus Christ; they will know that she is the most assured, the easiest, the shortest and the most perfect way to Jesus Christ, and they will devote themselves to her, body and soul and without reservation, in order to belong to Jesus Christ in the same way.

But who will be these servants, slaves and children of Mary?

They will be a burning flame, ministers of the Lord who will spread everywhere the fire of divine love.

They will be *sicut sagittæ in manu potentis*, sharpened arrows in the hand of powerful Mary for piercing her enemies.

They will be children of Levi, well purified by the fire of great tribulations and well attached to God, who will carry the gold of love in their heart, the incense of prayer in their spirit, and the myrrh of mortification in their bodies, and who will be everywhere the good scent of Jesus Christ to the poor and the little ones, whereas they will be the scent of death to the great, the rich, the proud and the worldly.

They will be thundering clouds, flying through the air at the slightest breath of the Holy Spirit, who, not attached to anything, not surprised by anything, not troubled by anything, will rain down the Word of God and life eternal; they will thunder against sin, they will rumble against the world, they will strike at the devil and his henchmen, and they will pierce again and again, for life and for death, with their two-edged sword of the Word of God, all those to whom the Most High will send them.

They will be true apostles of the last times, to whom the Lord of virtues will give the word and the power to operate marvels and bring back glorious spoils from their enemies; they will sleep without gold or silver and moreover, without care, among other priests, ecclesiastics and clerics, *inter medios cleros*; and nevertheless they will have the silver wings of a dove, in order to go, with the pure intention of God's glory and the salvation of men, wherever the Holy Spirit calls them, and they will leave nothing after them in the places they will have preached, except the gold of charity, which is the full accomplishment of the Law.

Finally, we know that they will be true disciples of Jesus Christ, walking in the footsteps of His poverty, humility, charity and detachment from the world, and teaching the narrow way to God in pure truth, according to the Holy Gospel, and not according to the wisdom of the world, without letting themselves be troubled, without making exception for anyone, without sparing, listening to or fearing any mortal, no matter how powerful he may be. They will have in their mouths the two-edged sword of the Word of God; they will carry on their shoulders the bloody standard of the Cross, the crucifix in their right hand, the Rosary in their left hand, the sacred names of Jesus and Mary upon their hearts, and the modesty and mortification of Jesus Christ in all of their conduct.

These are the great men who are to come, whom Mary will fashion by order of the Most High, to extend His empire over that of the impious, the idolaters, and the Muslims. But when and how will this happen? Only God knows; it is up to us to be silent, to pray, to sigh, and to wait: *Exspectans exspectavi* [I waited with expectation].

Chapter 3

Five Fundamental Truths

At this point, having discussed the necessity of devotion to the Most Holy Virgin, we must now discuss its substance. This I will do, with God's help, after I have presupposed some fundamental truths, which will bring to light this great and solid devotion I wish to reveal.

First Truth

Jesus Christ our Savior, true God and true Man, must be the final goal of all of our devotions, otherwise they would be false and deceptive. Jesus Christ is the Alpha and the Omega, the beginning and the end of all things. We work, as the Apostle says, only to render each man perfect in Jesus Christ, because it is in Him alone that all the fullness of the Divinity resides, along with all the other abundances of graces, virtues and perfections; because it is in Him alone that we have been blessed with every spiritual blessing; because He is our only Master who should teach us, our only Savior on whom we should depend, our only Head to whom we should be united, our only Model to whom we should conform, our only Physician who should heal us, our only Pastor who should nourish us, our only Way who should lead us, our only Truth in whom we should believe, our only Life who should vivify us, and our only All in everything who should suffice for us. There has not been given any name under Heaven other than the name of Jesus by which we must be saved. God has not laid for us any other foundation for our salvation, perfection and glory than Jesus Christ: every edifice that does not rest on this solid rock is founded on shifting sand, and sooner or later will inevitably collapse. Every faithful who is not united to Him like a branch to the vine will fall off, dry up, and become fit only to be thrown into the fire. If we are in Jesus Christ and Jesus Christ is in us, we have no damnation to fear at all; neither the angels in Heaven, nor men on Earth, nor the demons in Hell, nor any other creature can harm us, because they cannot separate us from the love of God which is in Jesus Christ. Through Jesus Christ, with Jesus Christ, in Jesus Christ, we can do everything: and we are thus enabled to give all honor and glory to the Father in union with the Holy Spirit, to render ourselves perfect, and to be to our neighbor the sweet scent of life eternal.

If therefore we firmly establish this devotion to the Most Holy Virgin, it is only to more perfectly establish devotion to Jesus Christ, it is only to provide an easy and assured way to find Him. If devotion to the Holy Virgin were to distance us from Jesus Christ, it would have to be rejected as an illusion of the devil; but completely to the contrary, as I have already shown and will demonstrate again in what follows: this devotion is not necessary to us except in order to find Jesus Christ perfectly, to love Him tenderly, and to serve Him faithfully.

I turn for a moment to you, Oh my dear Jesus, in order to lovingly protest to Your Divine Majesty that the majority of Christians, even the most learned, do not know of the necessary connection that exists between You and Your Holy Mother. You are, Lord, always with Mary, and Mary is always with You and could not be without You; otherwise she would cease to be who she is; she has been so transformed in You by grace that she lives no more, she is no more; it is You alone, my Jesus, who lives and reigns in her, more perfectly than in all the angels and the blessed. Ah! If men only knew the glory and the love that You receive in this admirable creature, they would have for You and for her many other feelings which they do not now have. She is so intimately united with You, that one could more easily separate light from the sun, heat from fire; I say moreover, one could more easily separate all the angels and the saints from You, than the divine Mary, because she loves You more ardently and glorifies You more perfectly than all other creatures together.

In light of all this, my dear Lord and Master, is it not astonishing and pitiable to see the ignorance and darkness of men here below with regard to Your Holy Mother? I am not speaking so much about the idolaters and the pagans, who, not knowing You, have no will to know her; I am not even speaking of the heretics and the schismatics, who have no will to be devoted to Your Holy Mother, having separated themselves from You and from Your Holy Church; but I am speaking of Catholic Christians, and even of Catholic theologians, who, while professing to teach the truth to others, do not know You or Your Holy Mother, except in a speculative, dry, sterile and indifferent manner. These gentlemen speak but rarely of Your Holy Mother and of the devotion one should have for her because they fear, or so they say, that someone might abuse it, that someone might offend You in honoring Your Holy Mother too much. If they see or hear someone who is devoted to the Holy Virgin speaking often of devotion to this good Mother, in a manner tender, forceful and persuasive, as an assured means without deception, a short path without danger, an immaculate way without imperfection, and a marvelous secret for finding You and loving You perfectly, they cry out against this person, and give him a thousand false reasons to prove to him that it is not necessary for him to speak so much of the Holy Virgin, that there are great abuses in this devotion, and that he should apply himself to destroying these abuses, and to speaking of You more often, rather than bringing people to a devotion to the Holy Virgin, whom they already love sufficiently.

One hears them from time to time speaking of devotion to Your Holy Mother, not in order to establish it or to persuade, but to destroy the abuses of it, even though these gentlemen are without piety and without tender devotion to You, because they do not have these for Mary; they regard the Rosary, the Scapular and Rosary beads as devotions of the weak, proper for the ignorant, and without which one can save oneself; and if someone who is devoted to the Holy Virgin comes their way, who recites the Rosary or who has some other devotional practice towards her, they will quickly change his spirit and heart; in place of the Rosary, they will recommend saying the seven psalms; in place of the devotion to the Holy Virgin, they will recommend devotion to Jesus Christ.

Oh my dear Jesus, do these men have Your Spirit? Do they please You in acting this way? Does it please You to not make every effort to please Your Mother, for fear of displeasing You? Does devotion to Your Mother hinder one's devotion to You? Does she keep for herself the honor one gives to her? Does she fashion a separate flock? Is she a stranger who has no connection to You? Does it separate or distance a man from Your love when he gives himself to her or loves her?

Nevertheless, my dear Master, the majority of intellectuals, as a punishment for their pride, would not distance themselves any more from devotion to Your Holy Mother, and would not act with any more indifference toward it, even if everything I just said were true. Keep me, Lord, keep me from their sentiments and their practices and give me some share in the sentiments of gratitude, esteem, respect and love which You have for Your Holy Mother, so that I may love and glorify You all the more as I imitate You and follow You more closely.

As if up to this point I had not said anything in honor of Your Holy Mother, give me the grace to praise her worthily: *Fac me digne tuam Matrem collaudare*, in spite of all her enemies, who are Your own, and I say to them forcefully with the saints: *Non præsumat aliquis Deum se habere propitium qui benedictam Matrem offensam habuerit*: The one who offends His Holy Mother cannot presume to receive the mercy of God.

To obtain from Your mercy a true devotion to Your Holy Mother, and to inspire the entire world with it, make me love You ardently, and receive for this end this ardent prayer which I offer to You with St. Augustine and with all Your true friends:

Tu es Christus, pater meus sanctus, Deus meus pius, rex meus magnus, pastor meus bonus, magister meus unus, adjutor meus optimus, dilectus meus pulcherrimus, panis meus vivus, sacerdos meus in æternum, dux meus ad patriam, lux mea vera, dulcedo mea sancta, via mea recta, sapentia mea præclara, simplicitas mea pura, concordia mea pacifica, custodia mea tota, portio mea bona, salus mea sempiterna... Christe, Jesu, amabilis Domine, cur amavi, quare concupivi in omni vita mea quidquam præter te Jesum Deum meum? Ubi eram quando tecum mente non eram? Jam ex hoc nunc, omnia desideria mea, incalescite et effluite in Dominum Jesum; currite satis hactenus tardastis; properate quo pergitis; quærite quem quæritis. Jesu, qui non amat te anathema sit; qui te non amat amaritudinibus repleatur... O dulcis Jesu, te amet, in te delectur, te admiretur omnis sensus bonus tuæ conveniens laudi. Deus cordis mei et pars mea, Christe Jesu, deficiat cor meum spiritu suo, et vivas tu in me, et convalescat in spiritu meo vivus carbo amoris tui, et excrescat in ignem perfectum; ardeat jugiter in ara cordis mei, ferveat in medullis meis, flagret in asbconditis animæ meæ; in die consummationis meæ consummatus inveniar apud te. Amen.

[You are, O Christ, my Holy Father, my merciful God, my infinitely great King, my Good Shepherd, my only Master, my Helper full of goodness, my Beloved whose beauty enraptures me. You are my Bread of Life, my Priest for all eternity. You are He who leads me home, my true Light, my holy sweetness, my

straight path, my Wisdom whose brilliance illuminates. You are
my simplicity full of purity, my peace and my gentleness, my
rampart, my inheritance, my eternal salvation... O Jesus Christ,
my Lord, why, during my life, have I desired anything else but
You, Jesus my God? Where was I when my spirit was far from
You? From this day forward, may I desire and long for nothing
but the Lord Jesus; may my heart grow in love for Him alone.
Desires that inhabited my life, flee from me now, for you have
tarried too long; hasten toward the fate that awaits you, look for
Him whom you truly seek. O Jesus, may the one who does not
love You be anathema! May he be filled with bitterness! Jesus,
full of gentleness, may You be the lover, the object of delight
and the admiration of every heart that consecrates itself to Your
glory, God of my heart and my inheritance. Jesus Christ, may
my spirit give in; may You Yourself be my Life; may there be
illumined in me the burning fire of Your love, may its flames
engulf me with divine fire, may it burn unceasingly on the altar
of my heart, may it embrace me to the core of my being, may it
totally consume me; so that finally, at my last day, I may appear
before You entirely transformed in Your love. Amen.]

I wanted to present this admirable prayer of St. Augustine in
Latin, so that those who understand Latin would recite it daily
to ask for the love of Jesus, which we seek through the divine
Mary.

We do not belong to ourselves, but totally and completely to
Him, as His members and His slaves, whom He purchased for
an infinite price, the price of His own blood. Before Baptism,
we belonged to the devil as his slaves, but Baptism rendered us
true slaves of Jesus Christ, who should live, work and die only to
produce fruit for this God-Man, to glorify Him in our bodies and
to allow Him to reign in our souls, because we are His conquest,
the people He has acquired, and His inheritance.

It is for this same reason that the Holy Spirit compares us to trees planted along the waters of grace, in the field of the Church, which must produce their fruit in due time; to the branches of a vine, of which Jesus Christ is the vine-stock, which must yield good grapes; to a flock of which Jesus Christ is the shepherd, which must multiply and produce milk; to good soil of which God is the plowman, and in which the seed multiplies and produces thirty-fold, sixty-fold, or a hundred-fold. Jesus Christ gave His curse to the barren fig tree, and will bring judgment against the useless servant who does not make the most of his talent. All of this proves that Jesus Christ desires to receive some fruit from our pitiful selves, namely our good works, because our good works belong to Him alone: *Creati in operibus bonis in Christo Jesu*: Created for good works in Jesus Christ. These words of the Holy Spirit demonstrate that Jesus Christ is the unique source and should be the unique end of all of our good works, and that we should serve Him, not only as His paid servants, but as His slaves of love. Allow me to explain.

There are two manners here below of belonging to another and of being dependent on his authority, namely: simple servanthood and slavery; that which we call a servant and a slave. In the servanthood common among Christians, a man promises to serve another for a certain amount of time, earning a certain wage or some other compensation. In slavery, a man is totally dependent on another for his entire life, and must serve his master, without claiming from him any wage or compensation, like one of his beasts over which he has the rights of life and death.

There are three kinds of slavery: natural slavery, forced slavery and voluntary slavery. All creatures are slaves of God in the first manner: *Domini est terra et plenitudo ejus* [to God belongs the Earth and its fullness]; the demons and the damned in the second; the just and the saints in the third. Voluntary slavery is more perfect and more glorious in the sight of God, who looks at the heart, and who asks for the heart, and who is called the God of the heart or of the loving will, because by this slavery one makes the choice, above everything else, for God and to be at His service, even though nature does not oblige it.

There is a complete and utter difference between a servant and a slave:

A servant does not give his master all that he is and all that he has and all that he might acquire by himself or from another; but the slave gives himself entirely to his master, including all that he possesses and all that he might acquire, without exception.

The servant demands wages for the services he renders to his master, but the slave cannot demand anything, no matter how diligent, how industrious, or how vigorous his work.

The servant can leave his master whenever he wishes, or at least when his term of service expires; but the slave has no right to leave his master when he wants.

The master of a servant does not have any right of life or death over him, such that if he were to kill him like one of the beasts in his charge, he would be committing an unjust murder; but the master of a slave has, by law, the rights of life and death over him, such that he can sell him to whomever he wants, or kill him, as he would his horse, without making any direct comparison.

Finally, the servant is at the service of a master only for a time, but the slave forever.

There is nothing among men that makes us belong to another more than slavery; there is nothing also among Christians that makes us belong so completely to Jesus Christ and to His Holy Mother as voluntary slavery, according to the example of Jesus Christ

Himself, who took the form of a slave for love of us: *Formam servi accipiens*, and of the Holy Virgin, who called herself the servant and the slave of the Lord. The Apostle was honored to call himself *servus Christi*. Christians are called several times in the Holy Scriptures *servi Christi*; the word *servus*, according to a truthful remark made by a great man, used to signify nothing other than slave, because there were not as yet servants as we have them today, masters being only served by slaves or freed slaves; that which the Catechism of the Holy Council of Trent, in order to leave absolutely no doubt that we are slaves of Jesus Christ, expresses by a term which is unequivocal, in calling us *mancipia Christi*: slaves of Jesus Christ.

Having established this, I declare that we ought to belong to Jesus Christ and serve Him, not only as His servants, but as loving slaves who, as a consequence of great love, give ourselves and deliver ourselves to serve Him as slaves, for the sole honor of belonging to Him. Before Baptism we were slaves of the devil; Baptism rendered us slaves of Jesus Christ; Christians must be either slaves of the devil or slaves of Christ.

Second Truth

That which I say in an absolute sense about Jesus Christ, I say in a relative sense about the Holy Virgin: that Jesus Christ, having chosen her as His inseparable companion during His life, at His death, in His glory and in His power in Heaven and on Earth, gave her by grace, relative to His Majesty, all the same rights and privileges that He possesses by nature; *Quid-quid Deo convenit par naturamn Mariæ convenit par gratiam*: that which is proper to God by nature is proper to Mary by grace, say the saints; in such a way that, according to them, both having the same will and the same power, they both therefore have the same subjects, servants and slaves.

One can, therefore, following the sentiments of the saints and of many great men, call oneself and make oneself the loving slave of the Most Holy Virgin, in order thus to be more perfectly the slave of Jesus Christ. The Holy Virgin is the way of which our Savior availed Himself to come to us; she is also the way of which we ought to avail ourselves to go to Him, because she is not like other creatures, to which if we were to attach ourselves, they could sooner lead us further away from God than closer to Him; but the most powerful inclination of Mary is to unite us to Jesus Christ her Son, and the most powerful inclination of the Son is that we come to Him by His Holy Mother; and this gives Him honor and pleasure, as it would give honor and pleasure to a king if, in order to become more perfectly his subject and his slave, one were to make oneself a slave of the queen. This is why the Holy Fathers and St. Bonaventure after them say that the Holy Virgin is the way to go to Our Savior: *Via veniendi ad Christum est appropinquare ad illam.*

In addition, if, as I have said, the Holy Virgin is the Queen and the Sovereign of Heaven and Earth: *Ecce imperio Dei omnia subjiciuntur et Virgo; ecce imperio Virginis omnia subjiciuntur et Deus* [all is subject to the power of God, even the Virgin; all is subject to power of the Virgin, even God], as say St. Anselm, St. Bernard, St. Bernardine, and St. Bonaventure, then does it not follow that she has as many subjects and slaves as there are creatures? Is it not reasonable that among so many forced slaves, there would be those who choose, as willing and loving slaves, to have Mary as their Queen? What? men and demons have their voluntary slaves, and Mary has none? What? a king considers it an honor that the queen, his companion, has slaves over whom she holds the rights of life and of death, because the honor and the power of one is the honor and the power of the other; and one could believe that Our Lord, who, as the best of all sons, shared all of His power with His Holy Mother, would object to her having slaves? Does He have less respect and love for His

Mother than Assuerus had for Esther and than Solomon had for Bathsheeba? Who would dare say this or even think it?

But where is my pen taking me? Why do I tarry here to prove such an obvious thing? If one does not wish to call oneself a slave of the Holy Virgin, what does it matter? Then one can make oneself and call oneself a slave of Jesus Christ! It is the same as being a slave of the Holy Virgin, because Jesus is the fruit and the glory of Mary. This is what one does perfectly by the devotion of which we will presently speak.

Third Truth

Our best actions are ordinarily defiled and corrupted by the evil foundation that is within us. When one puts clean, clear water in a vessel that has a bad odor, or wine in a container whose interior is spoiled by another wine it had contained, the clear water or the good wine is thereby spoiled and easily takes on the bad odor. In the same way, when God places into the vessel of our soul, spoiled as it is by original and actual sin, His graces and celestial dew or the delicious wine of His love, these gifts of His are ordinarily spoiled and defiled by the bad leaven and the evil foundation that sin has left in us; our actions, even those produced by the most sublime of virtues, smell of it. It is, therefore, of great importance, in order to acquire perfection, which cannot be acquired except through union with Jesus Christ, to empty ourselves of all that is evil within us: otherwise, our Lord, who is infinitely pure and despises infinitely the slightest defilement in a soul, will reject us from His sight, and will in no way unite Himself to us.

First, in order to accomplish this self-emptying, it is necessary, to know well, by the light of the Holy Spirit, our evil foundation, our incapacity to do anything beneficial for our salvation, our weakness in everything, our fickleness at all times, our unworthiness in every place. The sin of our first father has almost completely spoiled, soured, raised and corrupted us, as the leaven sours, raises and corrupts the dough to which it is added. The actual sins we have committed, whether mortal or venial, no matter how much they have been pardoned, have increased our concupiscence, our weakness, our fickleness, and our corruption, and have left an evil residue in our soul.

Our bodies are so corrupted, that they are called "bodies of sin", conceived in sin, nourished in sin, and capable of anything, bodies subject to thousands upon thousands of sicknesses, which corrupt themselves from day to day, and which produce nothing but mange, vermin and corruption.

Our soul, united to our body, has become so carnal, that it is called flesh; "all flesh has corrupted its way". Our lot is nothing but pride and blindness of spirit, hardness of heart, weakness and fickleness of soul, concupiscence, rebellious passions and sicknesses of the body. We are by nature prouder than peacocks, more attached to the ground than toads, meaner than goats, more envious than serpents, more gluttonous than pigs, angrier than tigers and lazier than turtles, more feeble than reeds, and more fickle than weathervanes. We have nothing at our foundation but nothingness and sin, and we merit nothing but the wrath of God and eternal hell.

After this, is it surprising that Our Lord said that whoever wishes to follow Him must renounce himself and hate his own soul; that whoever loves his soul will lose it and whoever hates it will save it? This Infinite Wisdom, who does not give commandments without reason, does not command us to hate ourselves except because we are so greatly worthy of hatred; nothing so worthy of love as God, nothing so worthy of hatred as ourselves.

Second, in order to empty ourselves of ourselves, it is necessary to die to ourselves daily; that is to say it is necessary to renounce the workings of the soul and the senses of the body, to see as if one could not see, to hear as if one could not hear, to avail oneself of the things of this world as if one did not have use of them, that which St. Paul called dying every day: *Quotidie morior*! If the grain of wheat that falls to the ground does not die, it remains in the dirt and produces no good fruit at all: *Nisi granum frumenti cadens in terram mortuum fuerit, ipsum solum manet*. If we do not die to ourselves, if the holiest of our devotions does not lead us to this necessary and fruitful death, then we will not produce any worthwhile fruit at all, and our devotions will become useless to us, all of our good works will be sullied by our self-love and our self-will; this will cause God to hold in abomination the greatest sacrifices and the best actions we can accomplish; and at our death we will find our hands empty of virtues and merits, and we will have not one spark of pure love, which is communicated only to those souls who have died to themselves, whose life is hidden with Jesus Christ in God.

Third, it is necessary to choose, from all the devotions to the Most Holy Virgin, that which leads us best to this dying to self, as this is the best and the most sanctifying type of devotion; because one should not believe that everything that shines is gold, that everything that is easy to do and is practiced by the greatest number is the most sanctifying. Just as there are secrets of nature for accomplishing certain natural processes in a short time, with little cost and with ease, there are likewise secrets in the order of grace to accomplish supernatural processes in a short time, with gentleness and with ease; to empty oneself of oneself, to fill oneself with God, and to become perfect.

The practice that I desire to bring to light is one of these secrets of grace, unknown to the majority of Christians, known to a few devoted ones, and practiced and appreciated by an even smaller

number. In order to begin to reveal this practice, here then is a
fourth truth which follows from the third.

Fourth Truth

It is more perfect, because it is more humble, not to approach
God by ourselves, without taking a mediator. Our foundation,
as I have just shown, is so corrupted, that if we rely on our own
works, skills and preparation to reach God and to please Him,
it is certain that all of our righteousness will be sullied, or of
little weight before God, in urging Him to unite Himself to
us and to hear and answer us. For it is not without reason that
God has given us mediators before His Majesty: He saw our
indignity and our incapacity, He took pity on us, and in order
to give us access to His mercies, He provided us with powerful
intercessors before his grandeur; in such a way that ignoring
these mediators, and approaching His Holiness directly without
any recommendation, is to lack humility, to lack respect towards
a God so exalted and holy; it is to think less highly of this King
of kings than one would of an earthly king or prince, whom one
would not want to approach without a friend to speak for him.

Our Lord is our Advocate and our Mediator of redemption before
God the Father; it is through Him that we must pray along with
the entire Church Triumphant and Militant; it is through Him that
we have access before His Majesty, and we must never appear
before Him except when relying on and clothed with His merits,
like the little Jacob with the goat skin before his father Isaac, in
order to receive his blessing [see Chapter 7].

But have we no need for a mediator before the Mediator Himself?
Is our purity great enough to unite us directly to Him, and by
ourselves? Is He not God, in every way equal to His Father, and
as a consequence the Holy of Holies, as worthy of respect as
is His Father? If, by His infinite charity, He made Himself our

ransom and our Mediator before God His Father so as to appease Him and to pay to Him that which we owe to Him, should we because of this have less respect and fear for His Majesty and His Holiness?

Let us therefore say heartily, along with St. Bernard, that we have need of a mediator before the Mediator Himself, and that the divine Mary is the one who is the most capable of fulfilling this charitable office; it is through her that Jesus Christ came to us, and it is through her that we must go to Him. If we fear to go directly to Jesus Christ who is God, either because of His infinite grandeur, or because of our lowliness, or because of our sins, let us heartily implore the help and the intercession of Mary our Mother: she is good, she is tender; there is nothing austere or rejecting about her, nothing too sublime or too brilliant; in seeing her, we see our pure nature. She is not the sun, which by the intensity of its rays could dazzle us because of our weakness; rather she is beautiful and gentle like the moon, which receives its light from the sun and tempers it to conform it to our limited grasp. She is so charitable that she never rejects anyone who asks for her intercession, no matter how sinful they may be; for, as the saints have said, never was it heard, since the world began, that someone was rejected who had recourse to the Holy Virgin with confidence and with perseverance. She is so powerful that never has she been refused in her requests; she has but to show herself before her Son in order to entreat Him: as soon as He receives her He concedes; He is always lovingly vanquished by the breasts and the womb and the prayers of His very dear Mother.

All of this is taken from St. Bernard and St. Bonaventure; so that, according to them, we have three stages to climb to go to God: the first, which is the closest to us and the most consistent with our abilities is Mary; the second is Jesus Christ; and the third is God the Father. To go to Jesus Christ, it is necessary to go to Mary, who is our mediator of intercession; to go to the eternal Father, it is necessary to go to Jesus, who is our Mediator of redemption. By the devotion that I am about to explain, one keeps this order perfectly.

Fifth Truth

It is very difficult, in light of our weakness and fragility, for us to maintain within us the graces and the treasures we have received from God, because we have this treasure, which is worth more than Heaven and Earth, in fragile vessels: *Habemus thesaurum istum in vasis fictilibus*, in a corruptible body, in a weak and changeable soul, which is troubled and disheartened by almost anything.

The demons, who are sly thieves, desire to surprise us so they can steal from us and rob us; they spy day and night for the most favorable moment to do this; they swirl about incessantly to devour us, and to take from us in one moment, by one sin, all that we have been able to gain in graces and merits over several years. Their malice, their experience, their cunning and their number should make us infinitely fearful of this misfortune, seeing that others more full of grace, more rich in virtues, more rooted in experience, and more advanced in holiness, have been surprised, robbed, and pillaged in the most unfortunate way. Ah! How many times has one seen cedars of Lebanon and stars of the sky fall wretchedly and lose all of their height and brightness in but a moment? Where does this strange change originate? It was not for want of grace, which no one is lacking, but for want of humility: they believed themselves to be stronger and more sufficient than they were; they believed themselves to be capable of protecting their treasures; they trusted in and relied on themselves; they believed their house to be secure enough and their coffers to be strong enough to protect the precious treasure of grace, and it is because of this imperceptible reliance they had on themselves (even though it appeared to them that they were relying solely on the grace of God), that the Lord, who is most just, permitted that they be robbed, in abandoning them to themselves. Alas! if only they had known the admirable devotion that I will bring to light in what follows, they would have entrusted their treasure to a powerful and faithful Virgin, who would have protected it as her own possession, and would have done this even as her righteous duty.

And finally, it is difficult to persevere in righteousness because of the strange corruption of the world. The world is now so corrupted that it is almost inevitable that religious hearts are soiled by it, if not by the mud, then at least by the dust; so that it is a kind of miracle when a person remains firm in the midst of this impetuous torrent without being carried away by it, in the midst of this stormy sea without being submerged in it or pillaged by pirates, in the midst of this poisoned air, without being polluted by it; it is this uniquely faithful Virgin of which the serpent has never had a part, who performs this miracle with regard to those who love her rightly.

Chapter 4

False Devotions

In light of these five truths, we must now more than ever make the right choice of true devotion to the Most Holy Virgin: for there are more false devotions to the Holy Virgin than ever, which can easily be mistaken as true devotions. The devil, like a counterfeiter and a sly and experienced deceiver, has already deceived and damned so many souls by false devotions to the Most Holy Virgin, that he avails himself daily of his diabolical experience to damn many others, in entertaining them and lulling them in their sin, under the pretext of a few badly recited prayers and a few exterior practices which he inspires in them. Just as a counterfeiter only counterfeits silver and gold, and very rarely other metals because it is not worth the effort, so also the evil spirit does not counterfeit other devotions as much as he does those to Jesus and Mary, i.e., devotion to the Holy Eucharist and devotion to the Holy Virgin, because they are, relative to other devotions, that which gold and silver are relative to other metals.

It is, therefore, most important first of all to recognize the false devotions to the Most Holy Virgin in order to avoid them, and to know the true one in order to embrace it; and second, among all the different practices of true devotion to the Holy Virgin, to know that which is the most perfect, the most pleasing to the Holy Virgin, the most glorious to God and the most sanctifying for us, in order that we might join ourselves to it.

I find seven kinds of false devotees and false devotions to the Holy Virgin, namely: critical devotees, scrupulous devotees, exterior devotees, presumptuous devotees, inconstant devotees, hypocritical devotees, and self-seeking devotees.

Critical Devotees

Critical devotees are, ordinarily, proud intellectuals, strong and self-sufficient spirits, who in reality do have some devotion to the Holy Virgin, but who criticize almost all those practices of devotion to the Holy Virgin that simple people offer in simplicity and holiness to this good Mother, because they do not fit with their imagination. They raise doubts about all the miracles and the stories recounted by authors worthy of faith, or taken from the chronicles of religious orders which have faith in the mercies and the power of the Most Holy Virgin. They can hardly bear to see simple and humble people on their knees before an altar or an image of the Holy Virgin, sometimes on a street corner to pray there to God; and they even accuse them of idolatry, as if they adored the wood or the stone; they say that they do not like these exterior devotions at all, and that they do not have such a weak spirit as to put faith in all the tales and stories that are told about the Holy Virgin. When one quotes to them the admirable praises that the Church Fathers have given to the Holy Virgin, either they respond that they were speaking as orators, by exaggeration, or they provide a bad explanation of their words.

These sorts of false devotees and prideful and worldly men are to be greatly feared because they do infinite harm to the devotion to the Most Holy Virgin, and very effectively cause people to distance themselves from it under the pretext of destroying its abuses.

Scrupulous devotees

Scrupulous devotees are those who fear dishonoring the Son by honoring the Mother, debasing the one by raising up the other.

They cannot tolerate it when someone gives to the Holy Virgin the fitting praises that the Church Fathers have given to Her; they can scarcely tolerate it when there are more on their knees before an altar of the Holy Virgin than before the Blessed Sacrament, as if one were contrary to the other; as if those who pray to the Holy Virgin are not praying to Jesus Christ through her! They do not want people to speak so often about the Holy Virgin or to speak so often to her.

Here are a few sentences that are typical for them: What is the good of so many Rosaries, so many confraternities and external devotions to the Holy Virgin? There is much ignorance in all of this! It makes a charade of our religion. Tell me instead about those who are devoted to Jesus Christ (they often name them without clarification, I might add parenthetically): we must run back to Jesus Christ, He is our only Mediator; we must preach Jesus Christ, that is what is most important.

In one sense what they say is true; but concerning the application they make of it, to hinder devotion to the Most Holy Virgin, it is very dangerous, and a sly trap of the evil one, under the pretext of a greater good; for never does one give more honor to Jesus Christ than when one honors the Most Holy Virgin, because one does not honor her except to more perfectly honor Jesus Christ, because one does not go to her except as the means to reach one's destination, which is Jesus.

The Holy Church, along with the Holy Spirit, blesses the Holy Virgin first, and Jesus Christ second: *Benedicta tu in mulieribus, et benedictus fructus ventris tui, Jesus* [Blessed are you among women, and blessed is the fruit of your womb, Jesus]; not because the Holy Virgin is greater than Jesus Christ or equal to Him, for that would be an intolerable heresy, but in order to more perfectly bless Jesus Christ, one must first bless Mary. Let us say with all the true devotees of the Holy Virgin, against the false, scrupulous devotees: O Mary, blessed are you among women, and blessed is the fruit of your womb, Jesus.

Exterior devotees

Exterior devotees are people who make their devotion to the Most Holy Virgin consist entirely of exterior practices; who appreciate nothing but the exterior part of devotion to the Most Holy Virgin, because they have no interior spirit; who say Rosaries hastily, attend many Masses without attention, take part in processions without devotion, enroll in all the confraternities without amending their lives, without subduing their passions and without imitating the virtues of this Virgin most holy. They like only the feelings of the devotion, without appreciating what is important; if they do not feel anything in their practices, they believe that they are not doing anything, they become distracted, they stop entirely, or they continue in fits and starts. The world is full of this sort of exterior devotee, and there are none more critical of those people of prayer who apply themselves to the interior aspects as the essential part, while not despising those modest exterior aspects which always accompany true devotion.

Presumptuous devotees

Presumptuous devotees are sinners abandoned to their passions, or lovers of the world who, under the good name of Christian and devotee of the Holy Virgin, hide their pride, or avarice, or impurity, or drunkenness, or anger, or swearing, or slander, or injustice, etc.; who sleep in peace in their bad habits, without practicing mortification in order to correct themselves, under the pretext that they are devotees of the Virgin; who promise themselves that God will pardon them, that they will not die without confession, and that they will not be damned, because they say the Rosary, because they fast on Saturdays, because they belong to the Confraternity of the Rosary or the Scapular, or to her congregations, because they wear the Scapular or the little chain of the Holy Virgin, etc.

When one tells them that their devotion is nothing but an illusion of the devil, and a pernicious presumption capable of causing them to be lost, they do not want to believe it; they say that God is good and merciful; that He did not make us to damn us; that there is no one who does not sin; that they will not die without confession; that a good *peccavi* [I have sinned] at the moment of death will suffice; what is more, they are devotees of the Holy Virgin; they wear the Scapular; they say every day blamelessly and without vanity seven *Paters* [Our Fathers] and seven *Aves* [Hail Marys] in her honor; that they even say from time to time the Rosary or the Office of the Holy Virgin; that they fast, etc. To confirm what they say and to make themselves even more blind, they carry around stories they have heard or have read in books, no matter whether true or false, and place their faith in the belief that there are those who had died in the state of mortal sin without confession, who, because during their lives they had said a few prayers or had done some acts of devotion to the Holy Virgin, were resurrected so they could make a confession, or their soul remained miraculously in the body until they could make a confession, or by the mercy of the Holy Virgin they obtained contrition and pardon for their sins from God at their death, and by this were saved; and so they hope for the same thing.

Nothing is more damnable in all of Christianity than this diabolical presumption; because can a man say that he loves and honors the Holy Virgin, while by his sins he unrelentingly stabs, pierces, crucifies and outrages Jesus Christ her Son? If Mary had made herself a law to save these sorts of men through her mercies, then she would have authorized the crime, she would have aided in crucifying and outraging her Son; who would ever dare to think such a thing?

I say that to abuse in this manner this devotion to the Most Holy Virgin which, after devotion to our Lord in the Most Holy Sacrament, is the holiest and the most solid, is to commit a horrible sacrilege, which, after the sacrilege of an unworthy reception of Communion, is the worst and the least pardonable.

I acknowledge that to be truly devoted to the Holy Virgin, it is not absolutely necessary to be so holy that one avoids all sin, although one should desire this; but one must at least (and listen well to what I am about to say): first, have a sincere resolution to avoid at least all mortal sin, which gives outrage to the Mother as much as to the Son; second, practice mortification and self-control in order to avoid sin; and third, become members of confraternities, recite the Holy Rosary or other prayers, fast on Saturdays, etc.

This is marvelously beneficial in the conversion of a sinner, even a hardened one; and if my reader is one such as this, with one foot in the abyss, I would advise him to do this, provided that he would not be doing these good works except with the intention of obtaining from God, through the intercession of the Holy Virgin, the grace of contrition and of forgiveness for his sins, and the grace to conquer his evil habits, and not to remain peacefully in his state of sin, in contradiction to his conscience, the example of Jesus Christ and of the saints, and the exhortations of the Holy Gospel.

Inconstant devotees

Inconstant devotees are those who are devoted to the Holy Virgin from time to time and in fits and starts; sometimes they are fervent and sometimes they are lukewarm, sometimes they appear to be ready to do everything in her service, and then, a little while later, they are no longer this way. They first embrace all devotions to the Holy Virgin; they join her confraternities, and then they do not faithfully follow the rules; they change like the moon, and Mary will put them under her feet, along with the crescent moon, because they are fickle and unworthy to be counted among the servants of this faithful Virgin, who have faithfulness and constancy as their nature. It would be better if they did not burden themselves with so many prayers and devotional practices, and instead did a small number of them with love and faithfulness, in spite of the world, the devil and the flesh.

Hypocritical Devotees

Then there are the false devotees of the Holy Virgin who are the hypocritical devotees, who cover their sins and their evil habits under the mantel of this faithful Virgin, in order to be considered in the eyes of men as something they are not.

Self-Seeking Devotees

Then there are the self-seeking devotees, who have recourse to the Holy Virgin only to win some court case, to avoid some peril, to heal a sickness, or for some other need of this kind, without which they would forget her; and these are also false devotees who have no standing before God or His Holy Mother.

Let us therefore be very careful not to be counted among the critical devotees, who believe nothing and criticize everything; scrupulous devotees, who fear being too devoted to the Holy Virgin out of respect for Jesus Christ; exterior devotees, whose entire devotion consists of exterior practices; presumptuous devotees, who, under the pretext of their false devotion to the Holy Virgin, wallow in their sins; inconstant devotees, who, because of their weakness, change their devotional practices, or quit them altogether at the slightest temptation; hypocritical devotees, who join confraternities and carry around books about the Holy Virgin in order to pass themselves off as being good; and finally, self-seeking devotees, who have recourse to the Holy Virgin only to be delivered from sickness or to obtain temporal goods.

Chapter 5

True Devotion

After having brought to light and condemned the false devotions to the Holy Virgin, it is necessary in a few words to establish the true devotion, which is interior, affectionate, holy, constant and unselfish.

First, true devotion to the Holy Virgin is interior, that is to say it proceeds from the spirit and the heart, it comes from the esteem one has for the Holy Virgin, from the high opinion one has of her grandeur, and from the love one has for her.

Second, it is affectionate, that is to say full of confidence in the Most Holy Virgin, like a child for his good mother. It causes a soul to have recourse to her in all its needs of body and spirit, with great simplicity, confidence and affection; it causes one to implore the help of this good Mother at all times, in all places and in everything: in one's doubts, to be enlightened; in one's straying, to be put right; in one's temptations, to be sustained; in one's weaknesses, to be strengthened; in one's falls, to be lifted up; in one's discouragements, to be encouraged; in one's scruples, to be freed of them; in one's crosses, labors and travails of life, to be consoled. Finally, in all one's maladies of body and spirit, Mary is one's usual recourse, without fear of bothering this good Mother or of displeasing Jesus Christ.

Third, true devotion to the Holy Virgin is holy, that is to say it inclines a soul to avoid sin and to imitate the virtues of the Most Holy Virgin, particularly her profound humility, her lively faith, her blind obedience, her continual prayer, her universal mortification, her divine purity, her ardent charity, her heroic patience, her angelic sweetness and her divine wisdom. These are the ten principal virtues of the Most Holy Virgin.

Fourth, true devotion to the Holy Virgin is constant, it strengthens the soul in goodness, it inclines it to not easily give up the practices of this devotion; it makes it courageous in opposing the world with its fashions and maxims, the flesh with its worries and passions, and the devil with his temptations; in such a way that a person who is truly devoted to the Holy Virgin is not the least bit fickle, gloomy, scrupulous or fearful. It is not that he does not fall or that the feelings he experiences in his devotion do not change from time to time; but if he falls, he picks himself up by taking the hand of his good Mother; if he loses his taste or his feelings for his devotion, he does not become troubled: because the just and faithful devotee of Mary lives by his faith in Jesus and Mary, and not by his feelings.

Fifth and finally, true devotion to the Holy Virgin is unselfish, that is to say it inspires a soul to never seek itself, but only God in His Holy Mother. A true devotee of Mary does not serve this august Queen out of a desire for gain or self-interest, nor for his own temporal or eternal well being of body or spirit, but only because she is worthy of being served, and God alone in her; he does not love Mary because she does good for him, or because he hopes that she will, but because she is lovable. This is why he loves her and serves her as faithfully during periods of spiritual dryness as during times of sweetness and feelings of fervor; he loves her as much on Calvary as at the wedding of Cana. Oh! how such a devotee of the Holy Virgin, who seeks nothing for himself in the services he offers to her, is pleasing and precious in the sight of God and His Holy Mother! But how rare such a person is today! It is in order to make this less rare that I take pen in hand to put down on paper that which I have taught fruitfully for many years in public and particularly in my missions.

I have already said many things about the Most Holy Virgin; but I have still more to say, and I will omit infinitely more, either by ignorance, insufficiency, or lack of time, in the plan I have to form a true devotee of Mary and a true disciple of Jesus Christ.

Oh! how worthwhile my effort would be if this little manuscript, falling into the hands of a well born soul, born of God and of Mary and not of blood, nor of the will of the flesh, nor of the will of man, would enlighten and inspire him by the grace of the Holy Spirit, to realize the excellence and the worth of the true and solid devotion to the Most Holy Virgin, which I will presently describe! If I knew that my criminal blood could serve to implant in his heart these truths which I write in honor of my dear Mother and Sovereign Mistress, of whose children and slaves I am the least, in the place of ink would I use it to form the letters, in the hope of finding good souls who, by their fidelity to the practice which I teach, would compensate my dear Mother and Mistress for the loss she has suffered due to my ingratitude and infidelity.

I feel myself enlivened more than ever to believe and to hope in everything I have engraved upon my heart, and which I have asked of God for many years, that is: that sooner or later the Most Holy Virgin will have more children, servants and slaves of love than ever, and that, through this, Jesus Christ, my dear Master, will reign in their hearts more than ever before.

I foresee many trembling beasts, who will come in fury to tear apart with their diabolical teeth this little manuscript and him whom the Holy Spirit has used to write it, or at least to envelop it in the shadows and the silence of a box, in order that it will never be seen; they will even attack and persecute those that read it and put it into practice. But so be it! So much the better! This vision encourages me and makes me hope for a great success, that is to say a great squadron of brave and valiant soldiers of

Jesus and Mary, both men and women, to combat the world, the devil and corrupted nature, in those perilous times which will come upon us more than ever before! *Qui legit, intelligat. Qui potest capere, capiat* [That the one who reads may understand; that the one who can understand may understand].

There are several interior practices of true devotion to the Most Holy Virgin, the principal ones of which are outlined here:

- Honor her as the worthy Mother of God, with the cult of hyperdulia, that is to say one should esteem and honor her above all the other saints, as the masterpiece of grace and the first in honor after Jesus Christ, true God and true man;
- Meditate on her virtues, her privileges, and her actions;
- Contemplate her grandeurs;
- Perform acts of love, praise and thankfulness for her;
- Invoke her lovingly;
- Offer oneself and unite oneself to her;
- Do all things with the goal of pleasing her;
- Begin, continue and finish all one's actions through her, in her, with her and for her, in order to do them through Jesus Christ, in Jesus Christ, with Jesus Christ and for Jesus Christ, who is our final end. We will explain this last practice.

True devotion to the Holy Virgin has also several exterior practices, the principal ones being:

- Enroll in her confraternities and enter her congregations;
- Enter into the religious orders founded in her honor;
- Make known her praises;
- Give alms, fast and practice spiritual and bodily mortifications in her honor;
- Wear her adornments, such as the Holy Rosary, the Scapular, or the little chain;
- Recite with attention, devotion and modesty the entire Holy

Rosary consisting of fifteen decades of *Ave Marias* in honor
of the fifteen principal Mysteries of Jesus Christ, or five
decades of the Rosary, which is a third of the whole Rosary,
in honor of either the five Joyous Mysteries, which are: the
Annunciation, the Visitation, the Nativity of Jesus Christ, the
Purification, and the Finding of Jesus Christ in the Temple;
or the five Sorrowful Mysteries, which are: the Agony of
Jesus Christ in the Garden of Olives, His Flagellation, His
Crowning with Thorns, His Carrying of the Cross, and His
Crucifixion; or in honor of the five Glorious Mysteries,
which are: the Resurrection of Jesus Christ, His Ascension,
the Descent of the Holy Spirit or Pentecost, the Assumption
of the Holy Virgin Body and Soul into Heaven, and her
Coronation by the Three Persons of the Most Holy Trinity.
One can also say a chaplet of six or seven decades in honor
of the years it is believed that the Holy Virgin lived on Earth;
or the Little Crown of the Holy Virgin, consisting of three
Paters and twelve *Aves*, in honor of her crown of twelve stars
or privileges; or the Office of the Holy Virgin, so universally
received and recited in the Church; or the Little Psalter of the
Holy Virgin which St. Bonaventure composed in her honor,
which is so tender and devout, that one cannot help but be
moved in reciting it; or fourteen *Paters* and *Aves* in honor of
her fourteen Joys; or other prayers, hymns and canticles of
the Church, such as the *Salve Regina* [Hail, Holy Queen],
the *Alma* [Alma Redemptoris Mater - Loving Mother of
the Redeemer], the *Ave Regina Cœlorum* [Hail Heavenly
Queen], or the *Regina Cœli* [Queen of Heaven], according to
the season; or the *Ave Maris Stella* [Hail Star of the Sea], *O
Gloriosa Domina* [Oh Glorious Mistress], or the *Magnificat*
[Mary's canticle, Luke 1:46-55], or other devotional prayers,
of which many books are full;

- Sing and inspire others to sing spiritual canticles in her
honor;

- Make a number of genuflections or reverences in her honor, by saying, for example, every morning sixty or a hundred times: *Ave Maria, Virgo fidelis* [Hail Mary, faithful Virgin], in order to obtain from God through her a faithfulness to God's graces throughout the day; and in the evening: *Ave Maria, Mater misericordiæ* [Hail Mary, Mother of mercy], to ask through her God's pardon for all the sins committed during the day;
- Work for her confraternities, decorate her altars, and crown and adorn her images;
- Carry and inspire others to carry her images in procession, and wear one as a powerful weapon against evil;
- Have images of her or inscriptions of her name made and place them in churches or in homes or at the entrances to towns, churches and homes;
- Consecrate oneself to her in a solemn and special manner.

There are many other practices of the true devotion to the Most Holy Virgin, which the Holy Spirit has inspired in holy souls, and which are very sanctifying; one can read about these at length in "Paradise Opened to Philagie", written by the Most Reverend Paul Barry, of the Company of Jesus, wherein he has collected a great number of devotions that the saints have practiced in honor of the Most Holy Virgin, devotions that have served marvelously for the sanctification of souls, provided they are practiced as they ought to be, that is to say: with a good and right intention to please God alone, to unite oneself to Jesus Christ as one's final goal, and to edify one's neighbor; with full attention, without voluntary distraction; with devotion, with neither haste nor negligence; with modesty; and with respectful and edifying bodily posture.

In these end times, I have encountered almost no devotion at all to the Holy Virgin. Above all, I affirm that, having read almost every book that discusses devotion to the Most Holy Virgin, and having conversed intimately with the holiest and most learned people of these end times, I have neither encountered nor learned of any devotion to the Holy Virgin similar to the one I wish to explain, which demands of a soul more sacrifices for God, which empties the soul more of itself and its self-love, which preserves the soul more faithfully in grace and grace in the soul, which unites the soul more perfectly and more easily to Jesus Christ, and finally which is more glorifying to God, sanctifying for the soul and useful for one's neighbor.

Since the essential aspect of this devotion is interior transformation, it will not be equally understood by everyone: some will stop at the exterior aspects, and not proceed any further, and this will be the vast majority; some, only a few, will enter into its interior aspects, but will only advance to the first level. Who will advance to the second? Who will achieve the third? Finally, who is the one who will be there by his very nature? The Spirit of Jesus Christ will reveal this secret to one such as this, and will Himself lead the truly faithful soul to advance from virtue to virtue, from grace to grace, and from light to light, to arrive at the transformation of himself in Jesus Christ, and the fullness of His age on Earth and His glory in Heaven.

Since our perfection consists entirely of our being conformed, united and consecrated to Jesus Christ, the most perfect of all devotions is without question the one that conforms, unites and consecrates us the most perfectly to Jesus Christ. And since Mary is, among all creatures, the most conformed to Jesus Christ, it follows that, of all the devotions, the one that consecrates and conforms a soul most closely to our Lord is the devotion to the Most Holy Virgin, His Holy Mother; and the more a soul is consecrated to Mary, the more it will be consecrated to Jesus Christ.

This is why perfect consecration to Jesus Christ is none other than a perfect and complete consecration of oneself to the Most Holy Virgin, which is the devotion which I teach; or, to put it another way, a perfect renewal of the vows and promises of Holy Baptism.

This devotion consists, therefore, of giving ourselves completely to the Most Holy Virgin, in order to belong completely to Jesus Christ through her. We must give her our body with all its senses and members, our soul with all its powers, our external possessions, which one calls our fortunes, both present and future, and our interior and spiritual possessions, which are our merits, our virtues and our good works past, present and future; in short, all that we possess in the order of nature and in the order of grace, and all that we can have in the future, in the order of nature, grace and glory, and this without holding anything back, not even one iota, one hair or the least good action, and this for all eternity, and without expecting or hoping for any recompense from our offering and service to her, except the honor of belonging to Jesus Christ through her and in her; and we would do all of this even if this loveable Mistress were not (yet she always is) the most generous and the most grateful of all creatures.

It is necessary here to point out that there are two aspects to the good works that we do, and they are: satisfaction and merit, or the satisfactory value and the meritorious value. The satisfactory value of a good work is the extent to which a good action satisfies the penalty due to sin, or obtains a new grace; the meritorious value, or merit, is the extent to which a good work merits eternal grace and glory. In this consecration of ourselves to the Most Holy Virgin, we give her all the satisfactory and meritorious value of all of our good works; we give her our merits, our graces and our virtues, not in order to communicate them to others (because our merits, graces and virtues are, to be precise, not communicable: it is only Jesus Christ who, in making Himself our ransom before His Father, could communicate to us His merits), but in order to preserve them for us; we give her our satisfactions, in order that she might communicate them to whomever she wishes, as she sees fit, and for the greater glory of God.

It follows from this: that by this devotion one gives to Jesus Christ, in the most perfect manner, because it is by the hands of Mary, all that one could give to Him, and much more than by means of any other devotions, by which one gives to Him either a part of one's time, or a part of one's good works, or a part of one's satisfactions and mortifications. Here everything is given and consecrated, even to the right of dispensing one's interior goods, and the satisfactions earned by one's good works from day to day: the same is not done even in religious orders. In a religious order, one gives to God one's fortune by the vow of poverty, one's body by the vow of chastity, one's free will by the vow of obedience, and sometimes one's freedom of movement by the vow of cloture; but one does not surrender the freedom or the right to dispense of the value of one's good works, and one does not strip oneself as much as one can of those most precious and valuable of Christian possessions, namely one's merits and satisfactions.

It follows that a person who has voluntarily consecrated and sacrificed himself to Jesus Christ through Mary can no longer dispense the value of any of his good works; all that he suffers, all that he thinks, says and does that is good belongs to Mary, so that she dispenses it according to the will of her Son, and to His greater glory, without, however, this dependence in any way hindering the obligations of one's present or future state of life: for example, the obligations of a priest who, by his office or otherwise, is obligated to apply the satisfactory value of the

Holy Mass to someone in particular; because one does not make this offering except according to the commands of God and the obligations of one's state of life.

It follows that one consecrates everything to the Most Holy Virgin and to Jesus Christ together; to the Most Holy Virgin as the perfect means through which Jesus Christ chose to unite Himself to us and us to Him; and to Our Lord as our final end, to whom we owe everything we are, as to our Redeemer and our God.

I said that this devotion could truly be called a perfect renewal of the vows or promises of Holy Baptism: because every Christian before his Baptism was a slave of the devil because he belonged to him. At his Baptism, by his own words or by those of his godfather and godmother, he solemnly renounced Satan, his pomps and his works, and he took Jesus Christ as his Master and Sovereign Lord, to become dependent on Him in the nature of a slave of love. This is what one does by this true devotion: one renounces (as it is written in the form of consecration) the devil, the world, sin and one's self and gives oneself completely to Jesus Christ through the hands of Mary [see the Appendix for a form of this consecration]. And one does even more than this, because in Baptism, one speaks ordinarily through the mouth of someone else, that is to say, the godfather and godmother, and one does not give oneself to Jesus Christ except by proxy; but in this devotion, it is personal, it is voluntary, it is a conscious decision.

In Holy Baptism, one does not give oneself to Jesus Christ through the hands of Mary, at least in any overt way, and one does not give to Jesus Christ the value of one's good works; one remains, after Baptism, entirely free to apply them to whomever one wishes or to keep them for oneself; but in this devotion, one gives oneself to Our Lord expressly through the hands of Mary, and one consecrates to Him the value of all of one's actions.

In Holy Baptism, says St. Thomas, men vow to renounce the devil and his pomps: *In baptismo vovent homines abrenuntiare diabolo et pompus ejus.* And this vow, says St. Augustine, is the greatest and the most indispensable: *Votum maximum nostrum quo vovimus nos in Christo esse mansuros (Epis. 59 ad Paulin).* This is also what the Canon Law writers say: *Præcipuum votum est quod in baptismate facimus* [the most important vow is the one we make at Baptism]. Nevertheless, who is the one who keeps this great vow? Who is the one who faithfully keeps the promises of Holy Baptism? Do not almost all Christians break the promise of fidelity they had made to Jesus Christ in their Baptism? What is the origin of this universal disorder, if not a neglect in living out the promises and pledges of Holy Baptism, and because almost no one personally ratifies the covenantal contract that he made with God through his godfather and godmother!

This is so true that the Council of Sens, convoked by the order of Louis le Debonnaire to correct the disorders of Christians, which were great, discerned that the principal cause of this corruption of morals was a forgetting and a neglect in living the pledges of Holy Baptism; and he found no better way of curing such a great evil than to bring Christians to renew the vows and promises of Holy Baptism.

The Catechism of the Council of Trent, the faithful interpretation of the intentions of this Holy Council, exhorts priests to do the same thing and to bring their people to recall and to believe that they are bound and consecrated to our Lord Jesus Christ as slaves of their Redeemer and Lord. Here are the words: *Parochus fidelem populum ad eam rationem cohortabitur ut sciat [...] æquum esse nos ipsos, non secus ac mancipia Redemptori nostro et Domino in perpetuum addicere et consecrare (Cat. Conc. Trid., pte I, c.3).*

So, if the Councils, the Church Fathers and experience itself shows us that the best way to cure the disorders of Christians is to get them to recall the obligations of their Baptism and to get them to renew the vows they had made, is it not reasonable to do this in a perfect manner by this devotion and consecration to our Lord through His Holy Mother? I say in a perfect manner, because one avails oneself, in order to consecrate oneself to Jesus Christ, of the most perfect of all means, which is the Most Holy Virgin.

One cannot raise the objection that this devotion is new or unimportant: it is not new, because the Councils, the Church Fathers and many authors, both ancient and modern, speak of this consecration to Our Lord, or renewal of the vows of Holy Baptism, as something practiced from of old, and which they recommend to all Christians; it is not unimportant, because the principal cause of these disorders, and by consequence of the damnation of Christians, is the forgetting of and the indifference toward this practice.

Some could say that this devotion, which causes us to give to Our Lord, through the hands of the Most Holy Virgin, the value of all of our good works, prayers and mortifications and almsgiving, leaves us powerless to come to the aid of the souls of our parents, friends and benefactors.

First, I would respond that it is inconceivable that our friends, parents or benefactors would suffer harm from our being devoted and consecrated without reserve to the service of Our Lord and of His Holy Mother. This would insult the power and the goodness of Jesus and Mary, who know full well how to help our parents, friends and benefactors with our tiny spiritual revenue, or by other means.

Secondly, this practice does not impede us from praying for others, whether living or dead, even though the application of our good works depends on the will of the Most Holy Virgin; on the contrary, it causes us to pray with all the more confidence; it is precisely analogous to a rich person who, having given all that he has to a great prince in order to bestow greater honor upon him, pleads with all the more confidence to this prince when asking him to give alms to a friend who requests it. This prince would no doubt take pleasure in having the opportunity to show his gratitude toward such a person who had stripped himself in order to clothe him, who impoverished himself in order to honor him. One must say the same thing about Our Lord and the Holy Virgin; they never let themselves be outdone in gratitude.

Again, one might say: If I give to the Most Holy Virgin the value of all my actions so she can apply them to whomever she wishes, it might be necessary for me to suffer longer in Purgatory. This objection, which comes from self-love and ignorance of the generosity of God and of His Holy Mother, self destructs. A fervent and generous soul, who puts God's interests above his own, who gives everything he has to God without reserve, in such a way that he can do no more, *non plus ultra*, who does not breathe except the glory and the reign of Jesus Christ through His Holy Mother, and who sacrifices himself completely to obtain it; regarding this generous and liberal soul, I ask: will he be more punished in the world to come for being more liberal and more self-denying than others? Far from it: it is to this soul, as we shall see in what follows, that Our Lord and His Holy Mother are most generous in this world and in the next, in the order of nature, grace and glory.

Chapter 6

Motives

We must now look, as briefly as possible, at the motives that make this devotion recommendable, the marvelous effects it produces in faithful souls, and the practices of this devotion.

The first motive shows us the excellence of this consecration of oneself to Jesus Christ through the hands of Mary.

If one can not conceive on Earth of a loftier employ than to be in the service of God; if the least servant of God is richer, more powerful, and more noble than all the kings and emperors of the world, if they are not servants of God, imagine the riches, the power and the dignity of a faithful and perfect servant of God who is entirely devoted to His service, without reserve and as fully as he could be! Such is the faithful and loving slave of Jesus in Mary, who has given himself entirely to the service of this King of kings through the hands of His Holy Mother, and who has kept nothing for himself: all the gold on Earth, all the beauties in the heavens could not repay him.

The other congregations, associations and confraternities established in honor of Our Lord and His Holy Mother, which accomplish such great good within Christianity, do not ask this surrender of everything without reserve; they prescribe to their members only certain practices and actions in order to satisfy their obligations; they leave them free in all their other actions and at all other times of their lives. But this devotion causes one to give to Jesus and Mary, without reserve, all one's thoughts, words, actions and sufferings, and every moment of one's life; in such a way that, whether awake or asleep, whether eating or drinking, whether doing the greatest works or the smallest, it is always true to say that whatever one does, even if one does not think about it, belongs to Jesus and to Mary by virtue of this offering, unless one has expressly retracted it. What consolation!

What is more, as I have already stated, there is no practice other than this one by which one rids oneself so easily of a certain possessiveness, which creeps imperceptibly into one's best actions; and our good Jesus gives this great grace as a recompense for the heroic and unselfish action one has done, in ceding to Him, through the hands of His Holy Mother, the complete value of one's good works. If He gives a hundred-fold, even in this world, to those who, for love of Him, give up worldly, temporal and perishable goods, what will be the hundred-fold He will give to the one who will sacrifice to Him even his interior and spiritual goods?

Jesus, our great friend, gave Himself to us without reserve, body and soul, virtues, graces and merits: *Se toto totum me comparavit*, says St. Bernard: He won me over entirely by giving Himself entirely to me; is it not a matter of justice and thankfulness that we give to Him all that we can possibly give? He was first generous toward us; let us be the same toward Him in return, and we will prove Him to be, during our life, at our death, and throughout all eternity, even more generous: *Cum liberali liberalis erit* [He will be generous with the generous].

The second motive will show us that it is just and advantageous to the Christian to consecrate himself entirely to the Most Holy Virgin by this practice, in order to be more perfectly consecrated to Jesus Christ.

This good Master condescended to enclose Himself in the womb of the Holy Virgin as a captive and a loving slave, and to submit and be obedient to her for thirty years. It is here, I say again, that the human spirit is overwhelmed, when it reflects seriously on this action of the Incarnate Wisdom, who did not desire, even though He could have done it, to give Himself directly to humanity, but instead through the Most Holy Virgin; that He did not desire to come into the world as a fully formed adult, independent of others, but as a poor and tiny baby, dependent on the care and the upbringing of His Holy Mother. This Infinite Wisdom, who had an immense desire to glorify God His Father and to save humanity, found no other more perfect or shorter way to do this than to place Himself in submission to the Most Holy Virgin in everything, not only for the first eight, ten or fifteen years of His life, like other children, but for thirty years; and He gave more glory to God His Father during this time of submission to and dependence on the Most Holy Virgin than He would have in using these thirty years to perform miracles, to preach everywhere throughout the world, to convert all of humanity; otherwise, He would have done so. Oh! oh! how one greatly glorifies God in submitting oneself to Mary, after the example of Jesus!

Having before our eyes an example so visible and so renowned throughout the world, are we so senseless as to believe that we could find a more perfect or direct way of glorifying God than that of submitting oneself to Mary, after the example of her Son?

Let us remind ourselves here, as proof of the dependence we ought to have on the Most Holy Virgin, of that which I have said previously, in recounting the examples that the Father, Son and Holy Spirit give to us of the dependence we ought to have on the Most Holy Virgin. The Father did not give and does not give His Son except through her, does not produce children except through her, and does not communicate His graces except through her; God the Son was not formed for all the world in general except through her, is not daily formed and brought forth except through her in union with the Holy Spirit, and does not communicate His merits and His virtues except through her; the Holy Spirit did not form Jesus Christ except through her, does not form the members of His Mystical Body except through her, and does not dispense His gifts and favors except through her. After so many convincing examples of the Most Holy Trinity, can we, without an extreme blindness, do without Mary, and not consecrate ourselves to her and depend on her to go to God and to offer ourselves in sacrifice to Him?

Here are several passages in Latin from the Fathers, which I have selected to prove that which I have just said:

Duo filii Mariæ sunt, homo Deus et homo purus; unius corporaliter; et alterius spiritualiter mater est Maria (St. Bonaventure and Origen). [Mary has two sons, a God-Man and a mere human; Mary is the Mother of the first in a corporal sense; and of the other she is Mother in the spiritual sense.]

Haec est voluntas Dei, qui totum nos voluit habere per Mariam; ac proinde, si quid spei, si quid gratiæ, si quid salutis ab ea noverimus redundare (St. Bernard). [This is the will of God, that we receive all through Mary; thus, if we have any hope, any grace, any salvific gift, we know that this has flowed to us through her.]

Omnia dona, virtutes et gratiæ ipsius Spiritus Sancti, quibus vult, quando vult, quomodo vult et quantum vult per ipsius manus administrantur (St. Bernardine). [All gifts, virtues and graces from the Holy Spirit are distributed by Mary to whomever she wishes, whenever she wishes, however she wishes and as much as she wishes.]

.

Qui indignus eras cui daretur, datum est Mariae, ut per eam acciperes quidquid haberes (St. Bernard). [You were unworthy to receive the divine graces; this is why they were given to Mary. Thus you receive through her that which you would not have received otherwise.]

God, knowing that we are unworthy to receive His graces directly from His hand, says St. Bernard, gives them to Mary, so that all He desires to give to us we obtain through her; and He also is glorified in receiving through the hands of Mary the thankfulness, respect and love we owe to Him for His goodness. It is therefore exceedingly just, says the same St. Bernard, that we imitate this conduct of God, so that grace might return to its Author through the same channel by which it came: *Ut eodem alveo ad largitorum gratia redeat quo fluxit.*

This is what one does through our devotion: one offers and consecrates all that one is and all that one has to the Most Holy Virgin, in order that Our Lord receives, through her mediation, the glory and the recognition He is due. One recognizes oneself as unworthy and incapable of approaching His Infinite Majesty by oneself: this is why one avails oneself of the intercession of the Most Holy Virgin.

In addition, this practice is one of great humility, which God loves over all the other virtues. A soul who exalts himself lowers God, a soul who humbles himself exalts God. God resists the proud and gives grace to the humble; if you lower yourself, believing yourself unworthy to appear before Him and to approach Him, He descends, He lowers Himself to come to you, to delight in you, and to lift you up in spite of yourself; but wholly to the contrary, when one boldly approaches God without a mediator, God takes flight, He cannot be reached. Oh! how He loves humility of heart! It is this humility that the practice of this devotion undertakes, because it teaches us that one should never approach God by oneself, no matter how gentle and merciful He may be, but always to avail oneself of the intercession of the Holy Virgin, whether to appear before God, or to speak to Him, or to approach Him, or to offer something to Him, or to unite oneself and consecrate oneself to Him.

The Most Holy Virgin, who is a Mother of sweetness and mercy, and who never lets herself be outdone in love and generosity, seeing someone give himself totally to her in order to honor her and to serve her, by stripping himself of all that he has that is most precious in order to adorn her therewith, gives herself totally and in an ineffable manner to him who gives her everything. She causes him to be swallowed up in the abyss of her graces; she adorns him with her merits; she supports him with her power; she enlightens him with her light; she embraces him with her love; she communicates to him her virtues: her humility, her faith, her purity, etc.; she gives herself and all that she has as ransom and as payment to Jesus. Finally, just as this consecrated person belongs totally to Mary, so also Mary belongs totally to him; in such a way that one can say of this perfect servant and child of Mary that which St. John the Evangelist said of himself, that he took the Most Holy Virgin unto himself: *Accepit eam discipulus in sua.*

This is what produces in his soul, if he is faithful, a great mistrust, contempt and hatred of himself, and a great confidence in and surrender to the Holy Virgin, his good mistress. He no longer places, as before, any trust in his own dispositions, intentions, merits, virtues and good works, because in having made a total sacrifice to Jesus Christ through this good Mother, he has but one Treasure wherein all his riches are found, and which is no longer within himself, and this Treasure is Mary.

This is what allows us to approach Our Lord without servile or scrupulous fear, and pray to Him with great confidence; this is what allows us to enter into the sentiments of the devoted and learned abbot Rupert, who, making reference to the victory that Jacob won against an angel, says these beautiful words to the Most Holy Virgin: O Mary, my Princess, and Immaculate Mother of a God-Man, Jesus Christ, my desire is to do battle with this Man, that is to say the Divine Word, armed not with my own merits, but with yours: *O Domina, Dei Genitrix, Maria, et incorrupta Mater Dei et hominis, non meis, sed tuis armatus meritis, cum isto Viro, scilicet Verbo Dei, luctari cupio (Rup. prolog. in Cantic).*

Oh! how one is powerful and strong before Jesus Christ, when armed with the merits and the intercession of such a worthy Mother of God, who, says St. Augustine, has lovingly vanquished the Almighty!

Because of the fact that, through this practice, one gives to Our Lord, through the hands of His Holy Mother, all one's good works, this good Mistress purifies them, embellishes them and makes them acceptable to her Son.

She purifies them of the stain of self-love, and of the imperceptible attachment to creatures which slips unknowingly into the best of actions. From the moment they enter her pure and fruitful hands, these same hands, which were never fruitless or lazy, and which purify whatever they touch, remove all that is spoiled or imperfect from the gift one presents to her.

She embellishes them by adorning them with her merits and her virtues. It is as if a peasant, wishing to gain the friendship and the goodwill of the king, were to go to the queen and present her with an apple, which is all he owns, so that she might present it to the king. The queen, having accepted this poor little gift from the peasant, places the apple in the middle of a large beautiful gold platter, and presents it to the king from the peasant; at this point, the apple, however unworthy it might have been in and of itself for presenting to a king, would become a gift worthy of His Majesty, because of the gold platter upon which it sits and the person who presents it.

She presents his good works to Jesus Christ; because in the end she keeps nothing for herself from what one gives to her; she faithfully gives everything to Jesus. If one gives to her, one gives necessarily to Jesus; if one praises her or glorifies her, she immediately praises and glorifies Jesus. Now, as long ago when St. Elizabeth praised her, she sings, when one praises her and blesses her: *Magnificat anima mea Dominum* [My soul magnifies the Lord].

She makes these good works acceptable to Jesus, however small and poor the gift may be for this Holy of Holies and King of Kings. When one gives something to Jesus, on one's own and depending on one's own industry and disposition, Jesus examines the gift and often rejects it, because of the self-love that stains it, just as long ago He rejected the sacrifices of the Jews, filled as they were with selfishness. But when one offers Him something through the pure and virginal hands of His Beloved, one gets Him at His weak spot, if one would permit me to use such an expression! He does not consider so much what is given as His good Mother who presents it; He does not look so much at the origin of the gift as to her through whom it comes. Thus Mary, who is never rebuffed, and is always well received by her Son, causes His Majesty to agreeably accept all that she presents to Him, whether small or great; it suffices that Mary presents it for it to be received and agreed to by Jesus. Such was the great advice St. Bernard gave to those whom he assisted on the road to perfection: When you wish to offer something to God, take care to offer it through the pleasing and most worthy hands of Mary, unless you want to be rejected: *Modicum quod offerre desideras, manibus Mariæ afferendum tradere cura, si non vis sustinere repulsam (St. Bernard, Lib. de Aquaed.).*

Is this not what nature itself inspires the little ones to do with regard to the great, as we have already seen? Why would grace not lead us to act in the same way with regard to God, who is infinitely higher than us, and before whom we are less than atoms? We have, in addition, an advocate so powerful that she is never refused, so industrious that she knows all the secrets of winning over God's heart, so good and generous that she never rebuffs anyone, no matter how insignificant or evil they may be. I will later describe the true prefiguring of these truths of which I speak, in the story of Jacob and Rebecca [see Chapter 7].

Faithfully practiced, this devotion is an excellent means of ensuring that the value of all our good works is used for the greater glory of God. Almost no one acts toward this noble end, even if one is so obligated, either because one does not know exactly what is the greater glory of God, or because one does not desire it. But the Most Holy Virgin, to whom one cedes the value and the merit of one's good works, knows perfectly what the greater glory of God is, and only acts for the greater glory of God. Thus a perfect servant of this good Mistress, who has consecrated everything to her, as we have said, can boldly say that the value of all his actions, thoughts and words is used for the greater glory of God, assuming that he does not expressly revoke his offering. Could there be anything more consoling for the soul who loves God with a pure and unselfish love, and who values the glory of God and His interests over his own?

This devotion is an easy, short, perfect and assured way of attaining union with Our Lord, wherein consists the Christian's perfection:

It is an easy way, a way that Jesus Christ opened up in coming to us, and in which there is no obstacle on our journey to Him. One can, in truth, attain divine union by other ways, but this would be through so many more crosses, so many strange dyings, and with so many troubles, that one could be victorious only with great difficulty. One would have to pass through many dark nights, through many strange combats and death throes, over steep mountains, through sharp thorns and across terrible deserts. But by the way of Mary, one passes through in a more gentle and tranquil manner.

In truth, there will still be great battles to wage and great difficulties to conquer; but this good Mother and Mistress remains so close and so ever present to her faithful servants, in order to illuminate them when they are in darkness, to elucidate them in their doubts, to strengthen them when they are fearful, to sustain them in their battles and difficulties, that in truth this virginal way of finding Jesus Christ is a way of roses and honey when compared to other ways. There have been a few saints, but small in number, like St. Ephrem, St. John Damascene, St. Bernard, St. Bernardine, St. Bonaventure, St. Francis de Sales, and others, who took this gentle path to go to Jesus Christ, because the Holy Spirit, the faithful Spouse of Mary, revealed it to them by a singular grace; but as to the other saints, who are far more numerous, although they all certainly had a devotion to the Most Holy Virgin, almost none of them entered into this way. It is for this reason that they had to pass through harsher and more dangerous trials.

Then why is it, a faithful servant of Mary might ask, that the faithful servants of this good Mother have so many occasions to suffer, and even more so than others who are not so devoted? They are contradicted, persecuted, slandered, and barely tolerated; or they walk in interior darkness or through deserts where there is not the least drop of dew from Heaven. If this devotion to the

Holy Virgin makes the way to Jesus Christ so much easier, why is it that they are the most crucified of all?

I would respond to him that it is certainly true that the most faithful servants of the Holy Virgin, being her absolute favorites, receive from her the greatest graces and favors from Heaven, which are crosses; but I would maintain that these servants of Mary are also those who carry these crosses with more ease, merit and glory; and that which would stop another over and over or make him fall, does not stop them even once, and causes them instead to advance, because this good Mother, totally full of grace and the anointing of the Holy Spirit, sweetens all these crosses, which she shapes in sugar and her maternal sweetness and in the anointing of pure love; in such a way that they swallow them joyously as if they were sweetened nuts, even though they would be by themselves very bitter. And I believe that a person who desires to be devoted to and to live piously in Jesus Christ, and by consequence suffer persecution and carry his daily crosses, will never carry great crosses, or will carry them neither joyously nor to the end without a tender devotion to the Holy Virgin, who is the sweetener of crosses: it is analogous to a person who is unable to eat, without extraordinary effort and then for only a short while, green nuts that are not sweetened with sugar.

This devotion to the Most Holy Virgin is a short way for finding Jesus Christ, either because one does not stray from the path, or because, as I have just said, one walks along it with more joy and ease, and consequently more swiftly. One advances more in a short time of submission to and dependence on Mary, than in many years of following one's own will and relying on oneself; for a man who is obedient to and in submission to the divine Mary will sing of his great victories over his enemies. They will want to impede his progress, or make him retreat, or make him fall, that is true; but, with the support, the help and the guidance of Mary, without falling, without retreat and without even slowing down, they will advance in giant steps toward Jesus Christ, by the same way as it is written that Jesus Christ came to us by giant steps and in but a short time.

Why do you think Jesus Christ lived such a short time on Earth, and in the few years He lived, spent almost His entire life in submission and obedience to His Mother? Ah! Having completed everything quickly, He did in fact live a long time, and longer than Adam, whose Fall He came to set aright, even though Adam had lived more than nine hundred years; Jesus Christ lived a long time, because He lived in complete submission to and unity with His Holy Mother, in order to obey God His Father; because the one who honors his mother is like a man who stores up, says the Holy Spirit, that is to say that the one who honors Mary his Mother even to submitting himself to her, and who obeys her in everything, will become very quickly rich, because he amasses daily treasures, by means of the secret of this philosopher's stone: *Qui honorat matrem, quasi qui thesaurizat* [the one who honors his mother is like the one who amasses a treasure]; because, according to a spiritual interpretation of these words of the Holy Spirit: *Senectus mea in misericordia uberi*: my old age is found in the mercy of the womb; it is in the womb of Mary, which enveloped and engendered a perfect man, and which had the capacity to contain the One whom the entire universe can neither comprehend nor contain, it is in the womb of Mary, I say, where the young man becomes old in knowledge, in holiness, in experience and in wisdom, and where he arrives in just a few years at the fullness of the age of Jesus Christ.

This practice of devotion to the Most Holy Virgin is a perfect way to advance and to become united with Jesus Christ, because the divine Mary is the most perfect and the most holy of all mere creatures, and because Jesus Christ, who came to us perfectly, did not take any other route than this for His great and wonderful journey. The Most High, the Incomprehensible, the Inaccessible, He Who Is, desired to come to us tiny earthworms, who are nothing. How did He accomplish this?

The Most High descended perfectly and divinely to us through the humble Mary, without losing anything of His divinity and holiness; and it is through Mary that the little ones must ascend perfectly and divinely to the Most High, without apprehension.

The Incomprehensible let Himself be perfectly enclosed by and contained in little Mary, without losing anything of His immensity; it is also through this little Mary that we must let ourselves be perfectly contained and led without hesitation.

The Inaccessible approached and united Himself closely, perfectly and even personally to our humanity through Mary, without losing anything of His Majesty; it is also through Mary that we must approach God and unite ourselves perfectly and closely with His Majesty, without fear of being rejected.

Finally, He Who Is desired to come to him who is not, and to make him who is not become God or He Who Is; He did this perfectly by giving Himself and submitting Himself completely to the young Virgin Mary, without ceasing to be in time the One Who Is from all Eternity; in the same way, it is through Mary that, although we are nothing, we can become like unto God, by grace and by glory, in giving ourselves to her so perfectly and so completely that we are nothing in ourselves and everything in her, without any fear of deceiving ourselves.

If one were to fashion for me a new way to go to Jesus Christ, and if this way were paved with all the merits of the saints, decorated with all their heroic virtues, lighted and embellished with all the luminous beauties of the angels, and if all the angels and the saints were there to guide, protect, and sustain those who desired to walk there; in truth I would boldly say, and I speak the truth, that I would rather take this way, which is so perfect, the Immaculate Way of Mary: *Posui immaculatum viam meam*: a path or way without the slightest spot or blemish, without original or actual sin, without shadows or darkness; and if my beloved Jesus, in His glory, comes a second time to Earth (which He certainly will) in order to reign there, He will not choose any other way for His journey than the divine Mary, through whom He so surely and perfectly came the first time. The difference between the first and the second coming is that the first was secret and hidden, and the second will be glorious and dazzling; but both are perfect, because both are through Mary. Alas! here is an incomprehensible mystery: *Hic taceat omnis lingua* [Let every tongue keep silent].

This devotion to the Most Holy Virgin is an assured way to go to Jesus Christ and to acquire perfection by uniting ourselves to Him; because this practice I am teaching is not new; it is in fact so ancient that one cannot precisely determine its origins, as was stated by Mr. Boudon, recently deceased in the odor of sanctity, in a book he composed about this devotion; it is certain, however, that beginning more than 700 years ago one finds evidence of it in the Church.

St. Odilon, abbot of Cluny, who lived around the year 1040, was one of the first to practice it publicly in France, as is noted in his biography.

Cardinal Pierre Damien recounts that in the year 1076, Blessed Marin, his brother, made himself a slave of the Most Holy Virgin Mary, in the presence of his director, in a most edifying manner; because he placed a cord around his neck and took on the discipline, and placed on the altar a sum of money as a sign of his devotion and consecration to the Holy Virgin, which he continued so faithfully during his entire life that he merited at his death to be visited and consoled by his good Mistress, and received from her mouth the promise of Paradise as recompense for his service.

Cesarius Bollandus makes mention of an illustrious knight, Vautier de Birbak, a close relative of the dukes of Louvain, who, around the year 1300, made this consecration of himself to the Holy Virgin.

This devotion was practiced by many individuals up to the 17th century, when it was made public.

Father Simon de Roias, of the Order of the Trinity, of the redemption of the captives, preacher of King Philippe III, brought this devotion into vogue throughout all of Spain and Germany; and obtained from Pope Gregory XV, through the entreaty of Philippe III, great indulgences for those who would practice it.

Father de Los Rios, of the Order of St. Augustine, devoted himself with his close friend, Father Roias, to spreading this devotion by his speaking and by his writings in Spain and in Germany; he composed a monumental work entitled: *Hierarchia Mariana* [The Hierarchy of Mary], in which he discusses, with as much piety as scholarship, the antiquity, the excellence and the solidity of this devotion.

The Theatin Fathers, during the last century, established this devotion in Italy, Sicily and Savoy.

Father Stanislas Phalacius, of the Society of Jesus, promoted marvelously this devotion in Poland.

Father de Los Rios, in his book mentioned above, recounts the names of princes, princesses, bishops and cardinals of different kingdoms who embraced this devotion.

Father Cornelius a Lapide, as commendable for his piety as for his profound knowledge, having received the commission from several bishops and theologians to examine this devotion, after having fully examined it, gave it praises worthy of his piety, and many other great men followed his example.

The Jesuit Fathers, always zealous in their service of the Most Holy Virgin, presented in the name of the Congregationists of Cologne a little treatise on this devotion to Duke Ferdinand of Bavaria, who was the archbishop of Cologne, who gave it his approval and the permission to have it printed, exhorting all the priests and religious of his diocese to promote this solid devotion as much as possible.

Cardinal de Berulle, whose memory is blessed throughout all of France, was one of the most zealous in spreading this devotion in France, despite all the slander and persecution he endured from critics and licentious men. They accused him of novelty and superstition; they wrote and published a defamatory pamphlet against him, and they, or rather the devil acting through them, made use of a thousand tricks to hinder him from spreading this devotion in France. But this great and holy man did not respond to their libel except with patience, and to their objections contained in their libel by a little tract in which he refuted them powerfully, in showing them that this devotion is founded on the example of Jesus Christ, on the obligations we have toward Him, and on the vows we made at our Holy Baptism; and it is particularly by this last reason that he silenced his adversaries, making them see that this consecration to the Most Holy Virgin, and to Jesus Christ through her hands, is nothing other than a perfect renewal of the vows or promises of Baptism. He said many beautiful things about this practice, which one can read in his works.

One can read in Mr. Boudon's book about the different Popes who have authorized this devotion, the theologians who have examined it, and the persecutions that they suffered and ultimately vanquished, and the thousands of people who embraced it, without a single Pope having ever condemned it, something which one could not do without overturning the very foundations of Christianity.

It remains, therefore, a given that this devotion is not new, and that if it is not common, it is because it is too precious to be tried and practiced by everyone.

This devotion is an assured way to go to Jesus Christ, because it is the very nature of the Holy Virgin to lead us assuredly to Jesus Christ, just as it is the very nature of Jesus Christ to lead us assuredly to the Eternal Father. And let not spiritual men falsely believe that Mary could ever be an obstacle to obtaining union with the Divine. Because, how could it be possible that she who found grace before God for everyone in general and for each person in particular, could be an obstacle to the soul seeking the great grace of union with Him? How could it be possible that she who was superabundantly full of grace, so united to and transformed in God that it was necessary that He became incarnate in her, could hinder a soul from being perfectly united to God?

It is true that focusing on other creatures, no matter how holy, could possibly, under certain circumstances, delay one's union with the divine; but not Mary, as I have said and will say forever without wearying. One reason so few souls attain the fullness of maturity in Jesus Christ is that Mary, who is as much as ever the

Mother of Jesus Christ and the fruitful Spouse of the Holy Spirit, is not formed sufficiently in their hearts. The one who desires to possess well ripened and well formed fruit should possess the tree which produces it; the one who desires to possess the fruit of life, Jesus Christ, must have the tree of life, which is Mary. The one who desires to have within himself the workings of the Holy Spirit, must have His faithful and inseparable Spouse, the divine Mary, who makes Him be fertile and fruitful, as we have said elsewhere.

Be therefore persuaded that the more you fix your eyes on Mary in your prayers, contemplations, actions and sufferings, if not with clarity and perception, at least in a general and imperceptible way, the more perfectly you will find Jesus Christ, who is always with Mary, in a great, powerful, effective and incomprehensible way, and more so than in any other place in the Heavens or in any other creature in the universe. Thus, far from the divine Mary, who is totally lost in God, becoming an obstacle to the perfect attainment of union with God, there has never been and there will never be another creature who will help us more efficaciously in this great work, either by the graces she will shower upon you for this purpose, no one being full of the thoughts of God except her, as a saint has said: *Nemo cogitatione Dei repletur nisi per te*; or by the protection she will provide against the illusions and the tricks of the evil spirit.

Where Mary is, the Evil Spirit is not; and one of the most infallible signs that one is led by the Holy Spirit, is when one has a great devotion to Mary, when one thinks often of her, and when one speaks often of her. This is the thinking of a saint who added that, just as breathing is a certain sign that the body is not dead, frequent thoughts of and loving invocations towards Mary are a certain sign that the soul is not dead from sin.

It is Mary alone, as state the Church and the Holy Spirit who guides it, who causes all heresies to perish; *Sola cunctas hæreses interemisti in universo mundo*; no matter how much the critics roar, never will a faithful devotee of Mary fall into heresy or illusion, at least formally; he might be able to fall into error, mistake a lie for the truth, and an evil spirit for a good spirit, though with much more difficulty than someone else; but sooner or later he will recognize his mistake and his error; and when he sees it, he will not stubbornly insist on believing in or maintaining that which he had believed to be true.

Whoever, therefore, without fear of being deceived, which is ordinary for people of prayer, desires to advance along the way of perfection and to assuredly and perfectly find Jesus Christ, he should embrace with his whole heart, *corde magno et animo volenti*, this devotion to the Most Holy Virgin, which he may not have known about before this. He should enter into this most excellent way, formerly unknown to him, but which I will show him: *Excellentiorem viam vobis demonstro.*

It is a way opened up by Jesus Christ, the Incarnate Wisdom, our unique head, a way from which a member of His Body cannot go astray. It is an easy way, because of the abundance of grace and the anointing of the Holy Spirit that fills it; one does not weary nor does one retreat while following it. It is a short way, which, in a short time, leads us to Jesus Christ. It is a perfect way, where there is no mud, no dust, not the slightest odor of sin. It is, finally, an assured way that leads us to Jesus Christ and to life eternal in a manner that is straight and assured, without diversion to the right or to the left. Let us therefore enter into this way, and let us walk there day and night, until the fullness of the age of Jesus Christ.

Since by this devotion one makes oneself a slave of Jesus Christ and consecrates oneself totally to Him in this capacity, this good

Master, as a reward for the loving captivity in which one places oneself, removes from the soul all scruples and servile fears which cause nothing but retreat, enslavement and confusion, enlarges the heart by a holy confidence in God, causing it to regard Him as Father, and inspires in the soul a tender and filial love.

Without stopping to prove this truth by reasoning, I will content myself with recounting an event that I had read in the Life of Mother Agnes of Jesus, a Jacobine nun, of the convent of Langeac in Auvergne, who died in the odor of sanctity in this same place in the year 1634. Being only seven years old and suffering great spiritual afflictions, she heard a voice who told her that if she wanted to be delivered from all her afflictions and be protected from all her enemies, she should, as soon as possible, make herself a slave of Jesus and His Holy Mother. No sooner had she returned to the house when she gave herself entirely to Jesus and to His Holy Mother in this capacity, even though she had known nothing of this devotion before; and, having found an iron chain, she placed it around her waist and wore it right up to her death. And after doing this, all of her afflictions and scruples ceased, and she found herself in a great state of peace and generous love, which motivated her to teach this devotion to many others who made great progress, among them Mr. Olier, a professor in the Seminary of St. Sulpice, and to several priests and clerics of the same seminary. One day, the Holy Virgin appeared to him and placed around his neck a chain of pure gold to bear witness to the joy she had that he had made himself a slave of Jesus and of her; and St. Cecilia, who accompanied the Holy Virgin, said to him: Happy those who are the faithful slaves of the Queen of Heaven, because they will enjoy true freedom: *Tibi servire libertas*.

That which should cause us all the more to embrace this practice is the great benefit our neighbor will receive from it. Because by this practice one demonstrates one's love toward him in a most eminent way, because one gives to him through the hands of Mary all that one has that is most precious, that is, the satisfactory and intercessory value of all one's good works, without excepting the smallest good thought or the tiniest suffering; one consents to the fact that all the satisfactions one has acquired or will acquire right up to the moment of death will be used, according to the will of the Holy Virgin, either for the conversion of sinners or for the deliverance of souls from Purgatory.

Is this not loving one's neighbor perfectly? Does this not describe the true disciple of Jesus Christ, who is recognized by his love? Is this not the way to convert sinners, without fear of vanity, and to deliver souls from Purgatory, without doing anything beyond that which one is obliged to do by one's state of life?

To truly know the excellence of this motive, it is necessary to know how much good is truly accomplished in converting a sinner or in delivering a soul from Purgatory: it is an infinite good, greater than the creation of the heavens and the Earth, because it gives to the soul possession of God. If, through this practice, one were to deliver but a single soul from Purgatory during one's entire life, or convert but a single sinner, is that not sufficient to urge every truly charitable person to embrace it?

But we must take note of the fact that our good works, passing through the hands of Mary, receive an increase of purity, and by consequence of merit and of satisfactory value; this is the reason they become so much more capable of soothing the souls in Purgatory and converting sinners, than if they had not passed through the virginal and generous hands of Mary. The little that one gives through the Holy Virgin, without self-interest and by an unselfish love, in truth becomes greatly powerful in lessening the wrath of God and attracting His mercy; and it may be that at his death a person who has faithfully followed this practice will find that he has delivered, by this means, many souls from Purgatory and converted many sinners, even though he did only those ordinary things required of him by his state of life. What joy at his Judgment! What glory in Eternity!

Finally, that which urges us more powerfully, in a certain respect, to practice this devotion to the Most Holy Virgin, is that it is an excellent way to persevere in virtue and in faithfulness. Why is it that the majority of conversions of sinners do not last? Why is it that one falls again so easily into sin? Why is it that the majority of the just, instead of advancing from virtue to virtue and acquiring new graces, often lose the small amount of virtue and grace they have? This misfortune comes, as I have previously shown, because Man, being so corrupt, so weak and so fickle, trusts in himself, relies on his own strength and believes himself to be capable of protecting his own treasury of graces, virtues and merits.

By this devotion, one entrusts to the Holy Virgin, who is most faithful, all that one possesses; and one accepts her as the universal trustee of all one's riches of nature and of grace. It is in her faithfulness that one places one's trust, it is on her power that one relies, it is in her mercy and her charity that one is grounded, in order that she might conserve and increase our virtues and merits, in spite of the Devil, the world and the flesh, who try their best to take them from us. One says to her, as a good child to his mother, and a faithful servant to his mistress: *Depositum custody* [Keep the deposit]. My good Mother and Mistress, I admit that up to this point in my life I have received more graces from God through your intercession than I deserve, and that my deadly experience has taught me that I carry this treasure in a very fragile vessel and that I am too weak and worthless to conserve these graces by myself: *adolescentulus sum ego et contemptus* [I am wretched and contemptible]; in your goodness, receive as a deposit all that I possess, and keep it safe for me by your faithfulness and your power. Because you keep me, I lose nothing; because you sustain me, I will never fall; because you protect me, I am impervious to my enemies.

This is precisely what St. Bernard said in a formal way, in order to inspire us in this practice: When she sustains you, you will not fall, when she protects you, you have nothing to fear; when she leads you, you will not grow weary; when she shows you her favor, you will make it safely to the harbor of salvation: *Ipsa tenente, non corruis; ipsa protegente, non metuis; ipsa duce, non fatigaris, ipsa propitia, pervenis (Serm. Super Missus)*.

St. Bonaventure seems to have said the same thing in a more formal way: The Holy Virgin, he says, is not simply preserved in the plenitude of the saints; but she preserves and keeps the saints in their plenitude, in order that it not diminish; she prevents their virtues from dissipating, their merits from perishing, their graces from being lost, the demons from harming them; finally, she keeps Our Lord from chastising them when they sin: *Virgo non solum in plenitudine sanctorum detinetur, sed etiam in plenitudine sanctos detinet, ne plenitudo minuatur; detinet virtutes ne fugiant; detinet merita ne pereant; detinet gratias ne effluant; detinet daemones ne noceant; detinet Filium ne peccatores percutiat (S. Bon. In Speculo B. V.)*.

The Most Holy Virgin is the faithful Virgin who, by her faithfulness to God, repairs that which was lost by Eve the Unfaithful in her unfaithfulness, and who obtains faithfulness to God and perseverance for those who cling to her. This is why a saint has compared her to a firm anchor, which holds them and prevents them from being shipwrecked in the tumultuous sea of this world where so many people perish due to their not holding onto this anchor: We attach, he says, our souls to our hope in you as to a firm anchor: *Animas ad spem tuam sicut ad firmam anchoram alligamus*. It is to her that the saints who are saved are the most firmly attached, and have attached others so that they may persevere in virtue. Happy then, and a thousand times happy, those Christians who now cling to her faithfully and completely as to a firm anchor. The attempts by the storms of this world will never cause them to sink, nor to lose their heavenly treasures. Happy those who enter into her as if entering into the ark of Noah! The flood waters of sin, which harm so many in the world, will never harm them, because: *Qui operantur in me non peccabunt*: those who are in me in order to work out their salvation will sin no more, she says with Wisdom. Happy the unfaithful children of miserable Eve, who attach themselves to this faithful Mother and Virgin, she who remains ever faithful and in whom there is no contradiction: *Fidelis permanet, se ipsam negare non potest*, who loves forever those who love her: *Ego diligentes me diligo*, not only with affectionate love but with effective and efficacious love, in preventing them, by a great abundance of graces, from retreating from virtue or from falling on the way by losing the grace of her Son.

This good Mother always receives, by pure charity, all that one gives her on deposit; and once she has received it on deposit, she is obligated by justice, because of the nature of a deposit, to keep it for us; it is analogous to the situation where, if I were to entrust a deposit of a thousand ecus to someone, he would be obligated to keep it for me, such that if by his negligence my thousand ecus were to be lost, he would by justice be responsible for them. But no, the faithful Mary would never allow what has been entrusted to her to be lost through negligence; Heaven and Earth would sooner pass away before she could be negligent and unfaithful towards those who place their trust in her.

Poor children of Mary, your weakness is extreme, your inconstancy is great, you are rotten to the core; you are taken from the same corrupted heap as all the children of Adam and

Eve; but be not discouraged by this; rather be consoled, and even rejoice: for here is the secret I am showing you, a secret unknown by most Christians, even the most devoted.

Do not leave your gold and silver in your safe boxes, which have already been broken open by the evil spirit who has robbed you, and which are too small, too fragile and too old to contain a treasure so great and precious. Do not place pure, clear water from the source into your vessels that are spoiled and infected by sin; even if the sin does not remain, its odor is still there, the water will be spoiled. Do not pour your exquisite wines into your old wineskins that had been filled with bad wine; they will be spoiled by it and will be in danger of spilling out.

Although you understand me, you souls who are predestined, I will speak even more openly. Do not entrust the gold of your charity, the silver of your purity, the waters of celestial graces, nor the wines of your merits and virtues to a bag with holes in it, to an old and broken safe box, to a spoiled and corrupted container such as you are; otherwise, you will be robbed by thieves, that is to say by demons who search and spy, night and day, the perfect time to do it; otherwise, you will spoil, by your bad odor of self-love, self-confidence and self-will, all that God gives you that is pure.

Place, pour into the womb and the heart of Mary all your treasures, all your graces and virtues; she is a spiritual vessel, she is an honorable vessel, she is a vessel worthy of devotion: *Vas spirituale, vas honorabile, vas insigne devotionis*. Ever since God in person enclosed Himself together with all His perfections in this vessel, it became totally spiritual and the spiritual abode of the most spiritual souls; it became honorable, and the throne of honor for the greatest princes of eternity; it became worthy of devotion, and the residence of those who are most illustrious in sweetness, in grace and in virtue; finally, it became rich as a house of gold, strong as a tower of David, and pure as a tower of ivory.

Oh! how blessed is the man who has given everything to Mary, who completely entrusts himself to and loses himself in Mary! He belongs completely to Mary, and Mary belongs completely to him. He can boldly say with David: *Haec facta est mihi*: Mary was made for me; and with the Beloved Disciple, *Accepi eam in mea*: I have taken her as my own, or with Jesus Christ: *Omnia mea tua sunt, et omnia tua mea sunt*: All that I have is yours, and all that you have is mine.

If some critic reads this and imagines that I am speaking in exaggeration and with excessive devotion, alas! he does not understand me, either because he is a carnal man, who does not savor the things of the spirit, or he is of this world, and cannot receive the Holy Spirit, or because he is too proud and critical, and condemns or mistrusts anything he does not understand. But those souls who are born not of blood, nor of the will of the flesh, nor of the will of man, but of God and of Mary, understand me and savor all that I am saying; and it is precisely for them that I am writing this.

However, I say for the one and for the other, in again taking up my subject after this interruption, that the divine Mary, being the most honest and the most generous of all pure creatures, never lets herself be outdone in love and in generosity; and for an egg, says a certain holy man, she gives an ox; that is to say, for the little that one gives to her, she gives abundantly from that which she has received from God; and as a consequence, if a soul gives itself to her without reserve, she gives herself to this soul without reserve, if one puts one's full confidence in her without presumption, working at her side to acquire virtue and master one's passions.

May the faithful servants of the Holy Virgin boldly say, therefore, together with St. John Damascene: "Having confidence in you, O Mother of God, I will be saved; with your protection, I have nothing to fear; with your help, I will vanquish my enemies; for devotion to you is an arm of salvation God gives to those He desires to save": *"Spem tuam habens, o Deipara, servabor; defensionem tuam possidens, non timebo; persequar inimicos meos et in fugam vertam, habens protectionem tuam et auxilium tuum; nam tibi devotum esse est arma quaedam salutis quae Deus his dat quos vult salvos fieri" (Joan. Damas., ser. de Annuntiat)*

Chapter 7

An Example from Scripture

Regarding all the truths I have just described about the Most Holy Virgin and her children and servants, the Holy Spirit provides us, in the Holy Scriptures, an excellent example in the story of Jacob, who received the blessing of Isaac his father through the care and skill of Rebecca his mother.

Here is how the Holy Spirit recounts it; I will follow with its explanation:

Esau, the eldest, had at one time sold his birthright to Jacob his younger brother. Several years later, their mother Rebecca, who tenderly loved Jacob, assured him in words both holy and full of mystery that he would receive this benefit. At the time, Isaac, realizing that he was very old and desiring to bless his children before he died, called to his son Esau, whom he loved, and ordered him to go and hunt down something to eat, in order that he might bless him afterwards. Rebecca alerted Jacob right away to what was happening and ordered him to take two kid goats from the flock. When he had given them to his mother, she prepared them for Isaac, knowing what he liked; she dressed Jacob in the clothes of Esau, which she had kept, and covered his hands and neck with the goat hides, so that his father, who could no longer see, would at least believe, despite hearing the voice of Jacob, that by the hair on his hands it was Esau his brother. Isaac, in fact, surprised by his voice, which he thought was the voice of Jacob, asked him to draw near, and touching the hair of the hides with which he had covered his hands, he said that although the voice was in truth that of Jacob, the hands were the hands of Esau. After he had eaten and, in kissing Jacob, had smelled the odor of his perfumed clothing, he blessed him and wished for him the dew of Heaven and the fruitfulness of the Earth; he established him as the master over all his brothers, and finished his blessing with these words: " Let the one who curses you be cursed himself, and the one who blesses you be filled with blessings."

Jacob had no sooner finished uttering these words when Esau entered and brought to eat what he had caught in the hunt, so that his father would then bless him. This holy Patriarch was surprised and greatly astonished when he realized what had just happened; but far from retracting what he had done, on the contrary, he confirmed it, because he rightly perceived the hand of God in what had happened. Then Esau began to wail in protest, as Scripture describes it, and loudly accusing his brother of deceit, he asked his father if he had but one blessing; he was in this way, as the Church Fathers remark, the image of those who, being totally at ease with mingling God and the world, desire to enjoy both the consolations of Heaven and those of the Earth. Isaac, moved by the cries of Esau, blessed him finally, but with an earthly blessing, and subjected him to his brother: that which caused Esau to conceive a hatred so vile toward Jacob, that he waited for nothing more than his father's death so he could kill him; and Jacob could not have avoided this death if his dear mother Rebecca had not protected him from it by her skillfulness and the wise counsel she gave him and which he followed.

Before explaining this story, which is so beautiful, one must note that, according to all of the Church Fathers and other interpreters of the Holy Scriptures, Jacob is the figure of Jesus Christ and the predestined, and Esau that of the damned. One has only to examine the actions and the conduct of the one and of the other to judge for oneself.

Esau, the eldest, was strong and of sturdy build, skillful and ingenious at the bow and at bringing home game from the hunt; he almost never stayed at home, and putting all his confidence in his own strength and skill, he worked only outdoors; he did not strive to please his mother Rebecca, and did nothing toward this end; he was such a glutton, and loved to eat so much, that he sold his birthright for a plate of lentils; he was, like Cain, full of envy toward his brother Jacob, and he persecuted him every chance he could.

And so the daily conduct of the damned: they trust in their own strength and skills for temporal affairs; they are very strong, clever and enlightened regarding earthly things, but very weak and ignorant of heavenly things: *In terrenis fortes, in cœlestibus debiles*. This is why they never, or almost never, remain at home in their own house, that is to say in their inner self, which is the house that God has given to each person as their interior and necessary dwelling place, following His example: because God always rests in Himself. The damned do not like retreating from the world, nor do they like spirituality or interior devotions, and they treat as weak in spirit, excessively devoted and uncivilized all those who are interior, and who are separated from the world, and who work more interiorly than exteriorly.

The damned rarely concern themselves with devotion to the Holy Virgin, the Mother of the predestined; it is true that they do not formally hate her, they praise her from time to time, they say they love her and they may even practice some form of devotion in her honor; yet they cannot tolerate it when someone loves her tenderly, because they do not have the fondness of Jacob for her; they criticize those devotional practices which her good children and servants faithfully undertake to win her affection, because they believe that this sort of devotion is not necessary for their salvation, and that, provided they do not formally hate the Holy Virgin or openly despise her devotions, then that is enough; and they believe that they have won the good graces of the Holy Virgin and are her servants, by reciting and murmuring a few prayers in her honor with neither tenderness for her nor amendment of their lives.

The damned sell their birthright, that is the pleasures of Paradise, for a plate of lentils, that is for the pleasures of the world. They laugh, they drink, they eat, they amuse themselves, they play, they dance, etc., without taking pains to make themselves worthy of the Heavenly Father's blessing, just like Esau. In three words, they think of nothing but the world, they love nothing but the world, they neither speak nor act except for the world and its pleasures, selling, for a tiny moment of pleasure, for a fleeting wisp of honor, for a morsel of gold or silver, their baptismal grace, their robe of innocence, their heavenly inheritance.

Finally, every day the damned hate and persecute the predestined, overtly or in secret; they overburden them, they despise them, they criticize them, they contradict them, they libel them, they rob them, they trick them, they impoverish them, they hunt them, they reduce them to dust; whereas they make their fortune, they take their pleasures, they have it easy, they enrich themselves, they make themselves great and live lives of comfort.

Jacob, the youngest, was slight of build, gentle and peaceable, and stayed ordinarily at home in order to win the good graces of his mother Rebecca, whom he loved tenderly; if he went out, it was not of his own will, nor by confidence in his own skills, but in order to obey his mother.

He loved and honored his mother, which is why he stayed at home with her; never was he so happy as when he saw her; he avoided anything that could possibly displease her, and he did everything he believed would please her; all this increased the love Rebecca had for him.

He was submissive in everything to his dear mother, he obeyed her completely in everything, quickly and without delay, and lovingly without complaining; at the slightest hint of her will, little Jacob ran and worked. He believed everything she said, without looking for a reason; for example, when she asked him to go and get two goats and bring them to her to prepare them for his father Isaac to eat, Jacob did not reply that one would have been enough to prepare for a single man to eat; without questioning, he did what she had told him to do.

He had a great confidence in his dear Mother; such that he never relied on his own knowledge, but relied solely on the care and protection of his mother; he went to her for all his needs, he consulted her in all his doubts; for example, when he asked her if, instead of a blessing, he would not receive a curse from his father, he believed her and trusted in her when she told him that she would take this curse upon herself.

Finally, he imitated as much as he could the virtues he saw in his mother; and it seemed that one of the reasons he stayed quietly at home was to imitate his dear mother, who was so virtuous, and to distance himself from bad company, which corrupts good morals. By this means, he made himself worthy to receive the double blessing of his dear father.

Here, then, is how the predestined conduct themselves every day: they stay quietly at home with their Mother, that is to say, they love to retreat from the world; they are interior, they apply themselves to prayer, following the example of and in the company of their Mother, the Holy Virgin, whose glory is completely within, and who, throughout her entire life, loved so much to retreat from the world to pray. It is true that they venture out from time to time into the world, but only in obedience to the will of God and the will of their dear Mother, in order to fulfill the duties of their state of life. Whatever great things they

accomplish outside, they esteem infinitely more that which they
accomplish within themselves, in their interior, in the company
of the Most Holy Virgin, because it is there that they are working
on the great work of their perfection, next to which all other
works are just children's games. This is why, although sometimes
their brothers and sisters work with much strength, skill and
success, with the world's praise and approval, they know by the
light of the Holy Spirit that there is much more glory, goodness
and pleasure in remaining hidden away with Jesus Christ, their
model, in a complete and perfect submission to their Mother,
than in performing marvels of nature and grace in the world
on their own, as did Esau and so many of the damned. *Gloria
et divitiae in domo ejus*: glory for God and riches for Man are
found in the house of Mary.

Lord Jesus, how lovely are your tabernacles! The sparrow has
found a home in which to stay and the turtle-dove a nest in which
to place her young. Oh! how happy the man who abides in the
house of Mary, where You were the first to make your abode. It is
in this house of the predestined where he receives help from You
alone, and where he has at his disposal all the virtues for every
stage of his life, in order to raise himself up toward perfection
from this valley of tears: *Quam dilecta tabernacula* [how lovely
is Your dwelling place].

They love tenderly and honor truthfully the Most Holy Virgin
as their good Mother and Mistress. They love her not only in
word, but in truth; they honor her, not only externally, but also
in the depths of their heart; they avoid, as did Jacob, all that
might displease her, and practice with all fervor all that they
believe will win her benevolence. They bring to her and give to
her, not two goats, like Jacob brought to Rebecca, but their body
and soul, together with all that depends on them, symbolized by
Jacob's two goats, so that: she receives them as something that
belongs to her; she kills them and makes them die to sin and to

themselves, in removing their own skin and self-love, and by this means, she pleases Jesus, her Son, who desires nothing for his friends and disciples except their dying to self; she prepares them according to the Heavenly Father's taste, and to His greater glory, which she knows better than any other creature; so that, by her care and her intercessions, this body and soul, well purified of every stain, well killed, well skinned and well prepared, would be a delicacy, worthy of the mouth and the blessing of the Heavenly Father. Is this not what those who are predestined will do, who will savor and practice the perfect consecration to Jesus Christ through the hands of Mary, which we are teaching to them, to manifest an efficacious and courageous love toward Jesus and Mary?

The damned say often that they love Jesus, that they love and honor Mary, but not from the depths of their being, not to the point of sacrificing their body with its senses and their soul with its passions, as do the predestined; they are submissive and obedient to the Holy Virgin, as to their good Mother, following the example of Jesus Christ, who, of the thirty-three years He lived on Earth, used thirty to glorify His Father by a perfect and complete obedience to His Holy Mother. He obeyed her in precisely following her advice, as did little Jacob in following that of Rebecca, to whom he said: *Acquiesce consiliis meis*: My son, follow my advice; or, like the guests at the wedding of Cana, to whom the Holy Virgin said: *Quodcumque dixerit vobis facite*: Do whatever my Son tells you. Jacob, because he obeyed his mother, received the blessing as if by a miracle, even though it was not due to him by nature; the guests at the wedding of Cana, because they followed the advice of the Holy Virgin, were honored by the first miracle of Jesus Christ, who there changed water into wine at the prayer of His Holy Mother. In the same way, all those who, until the end of time, receive the Heavenly Father's blessing and are honored with the marvels of God, do not receive these graces except as a consequence of their perfect obedience to Mary. The Esaus, on the other hand, lose their blessing due to their lack of submission to the Holy Virgin.

The predestined have great confidence in the goodness and the power of the Most Holy Virgin, their good Mother; they ask her unceasingly for help; they look upon her as their North Star, which guides them to safe harbor; they share with her their troubles and their needs with great openness of heart; they cling to her breasts full of mercy and sweetness, in order to obtain pardon for their sins through her intercession or to taste of her maternal sweetness in their troubles and worries. They even throw themselves into, hide themselves in, and lose themselves in her loving and virginal womb in a most wonderful way, to be embraced by pure love, and to be purified there from even the slightest blemish, and there to find Jesus in all His fullness, where He resides as if on His most glorious throne. Oh! what happiness! Do not believe, says Guerric the abbot, that there is more happiness to live in the bosom of Abraham than in the womb of Mary, because it is there that the Lord has set up His throne: *Ne credideris majoris esse felicitatis habitare in sinu Abrahae quam in sinu Mariae, cum in eo Dominus posuerit thronum suum.*

The damned, on the other hand, placing all their confidence in themselves, eating nothing, like the Prodigal Son, except that which the pigs eat, nourishing themselves on nothing, like toads, except the dirt, and loving nothing, like the worldly, except things visible and exterior, they never taste the sweetness of the womb and the breasts of Mary; they do not have that sure reliance and confidence that the predestined have for the Holy Virgin, their good Mother. They stay outside and wallow miserably in their hunger, as St. Gregory said, because they do not wish to taste the sweetness that has been fully prepared within themselves and within Jesus and Mary.

Finally, the predestined keep the ways of the Holy Virgin, their good Mother, that is: they imitate her, and it is in this that they are truly happy and devoted, and demonstrate the infallible sign of their predestination, as this good Mother says to them: *Beati qui custodiunt vias meas*: that is, blessed are they who practice my virtues and walk in my footsteps, with the aid of divine grace. They are happy in this world during their life, through the abundance of graces and sweetness that I communicate to them from my fullness, and more abundantly than others who do not so closely imitate me; they are happy at their death, which is gentle and tranquil, and at which I am ordinarily present, in order to lead them myself into the joys of eternity; finally, they will be happy in eternity, because never has one of my good servants been lost, who has imitated my virtues during his life.

The damned, on the contrary, are unhappy during their life, at their death and in eternity, because they never imitate the Most Holy Virgin in her virtues, contenting themselves with occasionally joining her confraternities, saying a few prayers in her honor or doing some other exterior devotion.

O Holy Virgin, my good Mother, how happy are they, I repeat with all my heart, how happy are they who, not allowing themselves to be seduced by false devotion to you, faithfully keep your ways, your counsels and your commands! But how unhappy and cursed are they who, abusing your devotion, do not keep your Son's commandments: *Maledicti omnes qui declinant a mandatis tuis*.

Here then are the loving favors that the Holy Virgin, as the best of all mothers, does for her faithful servants who have given themselves to her in the manner of which I have spoken, and following the example of Jacob:

Ego diligentes me diligo: I love those who love me. She loves them: because she is their true Mother: a mother always loves her own child, the fruit of her womb; she loves them out of gratitude, because they love her in fact as their good Mother; she loves them because, being predestined, God loves them; she loves them because they are consecrated to her, and they are her portion and her inheritance: *In Israel hœreditare.*

She loves them tenderly, and more tenderly than all other mothers combined. Put, if you can, all the natural love that all the mothers of the world have for their children, into the single heart of a mother for her only child; certainly, this mother would have great love for this child; however, in truth, Mary's love for her children is even greater than this mother's love would be.

She does not love them only with affection, but with efficacy. Her love for them is active and effective, like that of Rebecca for Jacob, and even more so. Here is what this good Mother, of whom Rebecca is but the prefiguring, does to obtain for her children the blessing of the Heavenly Father:

She watches, like Rebecca, for favorable opportunities to do good for them, to make them grow and to enrich them. Since in God she sees clearly all the good and the bad, good fortunes and bad fortunes, God's blessings and His curses, she arranges things from afar to exempt her servants from all sorts of evil and to fill them up with all sorts of good; in such a way that if there is a good fortune to be made in God by the faithfulness of a creature to some worthy endeavor, it is certain that Mary will procure this good fortune for one of her good children and servants, and provide them with the grace to succeed in it with fidelity: *Ipsa procurat negotia nostra* [she looks after our interests], said a saint.

She gives them good advice, like Rebecca did for Jacob: *Fili me, acquiesce consiliis meis*: My son, follow my advice. And, among other counsels, she inspires them to bring two goats to her, that is to say their body and soul, to consecrate them to her in order to make of them a ragout that is pleasing to God, and to do all that Jesus Christ, her Son, has taught by His word and example. If it is not she herself who provides this advice to them, then it is given through the ministry of angels, who have no greater honor and pleasure than to obey one of her commands to descend to Earth and come to the aid of one of her servants.

When one has brought to her and consecrated to her one's body and soul and all that depends on them, without exception, what does this good Mother do? That which Rebecca did long ago with the two goats that Jacob brought to her: she kills them and makes them die to the life of the old Adam; she skins them and removes their natural skin, their natural inclinations, their self-love and self-will and all worldly attachments; she purifies them of their blemishes and impurities and sins; she prepares them according to God's taste and for His greater glory. Since it is she alone who knows perfectly the divine taste and the greater glory of the Most High, it is she alone who, without error, can adapt and prepare our body and soul for this infinitely high taste and this infinitely hidden glory.

Having received the perfect offering we have made to her of ourselves and our own merits and satisfactions by the devotion of which I speak, and having shed our old clothing, this good Mother washes us and makes us worthy to appear before our Heavenly Father. She clothes us in the clean, new, expensive and perfumed clothing of Esau the first-born, that is to say, of Jesus Christ, her Son, whom she keeps in her home, that is to say whose power she has, being the universal and eternal treasurer and dispenser of the merits and the virtues of her Son, Jesus

Christ, which she gives and communicates to whomever she wishes, whenever she wishes, however she wishes, and as much as she wishes, as we have already seen.

She surrounds the neck and the hands of her servants with the skin of slaughtered goats; that is to say, she adorns them with the merits and the value of their own actions. She kills and mortifies, in truth, all that is impure and imperfect within them; but she neither loses nor wastes any of the good that grace has accomplished there; she keeps it and augments it to make it the adornment and the strength of their neck and their hands, that is, to strengthen them for carrying the Lord's yoke, which is carried on the neck, and to accomplish great things for the glory of God and the salvation of their poor brothers.

She gives a new perfume and a new grace to their clothing and adornments in giving them her own clothing. She gives them her merits and virtues, which she left to them at her death, according to her own will and testament, as a holy religious woman of the last century, who died in the odor of sanctity, had said, and who knew this by private revelation. She does this so that all of her faithful household servants and slaves are doubly clothed, with her Son's clothing and with her own: *Omnes domestici ejus vestiti sunt duplicibus*; this is why they have nothing to fear of the coldness of Jesus Christ, white like the snow, which the damned who are totally naked and stripped of the merits of Jesus Christ and the Holy Virgin cannot endure.

She enables them to obtain the blessing of the Heavenly Father, even though, being but the younger, adopted children, they have no inherent right to it. With their brand new, costly and well-perfumed clothing, with their body and soul well prepared and readied, they confidently approach the bed of their Heavenly Father. He hears and distinguishes their voice, which is that of a sinner; He touches their hands covered with hides and smells the sweet odor of their clothing; He eats with joy that which Mary, their Mother, has prepared for Him. And recognizing in them the merits and sweet odor of His Son and His Holy Mother, He gives them His double blessing: the blessing of the dew of Heaven: *De rore cœlesti*, that is to say divine grace, which is the seed of glory: *Benedixit nos omni benedictione spirituali in Christo Jesu*; and the blessing of the fat of the earth: *De pinguedine terrae*, that is to say, this good Father gives them their daily bread and a sufficient abundance of the goods of this world. He makes them masters over their other brothers, the damned; not that this primacy is always evident in this world, which passes in an instant, where often the damned are the rulers: *Peccatores effabuntur et gloriabuntur. Vidi impium superexaltatum et elevatum*, but nevertheless it is true and will be manifest in the world to come for all eternity, where the just, as the Holy Spirit attests, will have dominion and rule over the nations: *Dominabuntur populis*. His Majesty, not content with blessing them in their persons and in their belongings, also blesses those who bless them, and curses those who curse and persecute them.

The second charitable favor that the Holy Virgin does for her faithful servants is that she provides everything they need for the body and the soul. She gives them double clothing, as we have just seen; she gives them to eat of the most exquisite delights from the table of God; she gives them to eat of the Bread of Life, whom she formed; *A generationibus meis implemeni*: my dear children, she says to them under the name of Wisdom, fill yourself with my offspring, that is to say Jesus, the Fruit of Life, whom I brought forth into the world for you. *Venite, comedite panem meum et bibite vinum quod miscui vobis; comedite, et bibite, et inebriamini, carissimi*: Come, she says again to them in another place, eat my bread, which is Jesus, and drink the wine of His love, which I have mixed together with the milk of my breasts. As the treasurer and the dispenser of the gifts and the graces of the Most High, she gives a good portion, and the best, to nourish and sustain her children and servants. They are fattened on the Living Bread, they are inebriated on the Wine which brings forth virgins. They are carried at the breast: *Ad ubera portabimini*. They have such ease at carrying the yoke of Jesus Christ that they hardly feel its weight at all, because of the oil of devotion, which lightens it: *Jugum eorum putrescere faciet a facie olei*.

The third favor that the Holy Virgin does for her faithful servants, is that she leads and guides them according to the will of her Son. Rebecca led her little Jacob and gave him good opinions from time to time, either to draw upon him the blessing of his father, or to avoid the hatred and the persecution of his brother Esau. Mary, who is the Star of the Sea, leads all her faithful servants to safe harbor; she shows them the ways of life eternal; she enables them to avoid taking dangerous steps; she leads them by the hand in the paths of justice; she holds them up when they are about to fall and picks them up if they do fall; she takes them back, as a loving mother, when they wander off; and sometimes she even lovingly chastises them. Could an obedient child of Mary, his nourishing Mother and illuminating guide, stray from the way that leads to eternity? *Ipsam sequens, non devias*: In following her, says St. Bernard, you will never stray. Do not be afraid that a true child of Mary could ever be deceived by the evil one and fall into formal heresy. Wherever the guidance of Mary is to be found, neither the evil spirit with his illusions, nor the heretics with their shrewdness, are to be found. *Ipsa tenente, non corruis*.

The fourth good service that the Holy Virgin renders to her children and faithful servants, is that she defends and protects them from their enemies. Rebecca, by her care and skill, delivered Jacob from all the dangers he faced, and particularly from the death his brother apparently had in store for him due to the hatred and the envy he carried, as long ago happened with Cain and Abel. Mary, the good Mother of the predestined, hides them in the shelter of her wings, like a hen her chicks; she speaks to them, she stoops down to them, she condescends to help them in all their weaknesses; in order to protect them from the sparrow-hawk and the vulture, she surrounds them and accompanies them like an army arrayed for battle; *ut castorum acies ordinata.* Would a man surrounded and protected by an army of 100,000 men fear his enemies? A faithful servant of Mary, surrounded by her protection and her imperial power, has even less to fear. This good Mother and powerful Princess of Heaven would dispatch with haste battalions of millions of angels to come to the aid of just one of her servants, so that never could it be said that a faithful servant of Mary, who had relied on her, succumbed to evil because of the number and strength of his enemies.

Finally, the fifth and the greatest good that the benevolent Mary procures for her faithful followers, is that she intercedes for them before her Son, appeases Him by her prayers, unites them to Him by an intimate bond, and keeps them there. Rebecca convinced Jacob to approach the bed of his father; and this good man touched him, embraced him, and even kissed him with joy, being content and satiated with the well prepared meat he had brought to him; and having smelled contentedly the exquisite perfumes of his clothing, he cried out: *Ecce odor filii mei sicut odor agri pleni, cui benedixit Dominus*: Here is the scent of my son, which is like the scent of a flourishing field, which the Lord has blessed. This scent of the flourishing field, which charmed the heart of the father, is nothing more than the scent of the virtues and the merits of Mary, who is a field flourishing with grace, where God the Father has sown His only Son, like a grain of the wheat of the elect.

Oh! how a child perfumed with the good scent of Mary is welcomed by Jesus Christ, who is the Father of the world to come! Oh! how quickly and perfectly he is united to Him! We have shown this at length in the preceding pages.

What is more, having filled her children and faithful servants with her favors, and having obtained for them the Heavenly Father's blessing and union with Jesus Christ, she preserves them in Jesus Christ and Jesus Christ in them; she keeps them and watches over them always, so that they do not lose the grace of God and do not fall into the traps of their enemies: *In plenitudine sanctos detinet*: She maintains the saints in their fullness, and enables them to persevere to the end, as we have seen.

This, then, is the explanation of this great and ancient prefiguring of predestination and damnation, so unknown and so full of mysteries.

Chapter 8

Effects

My dear brother, be persuaded that if you faithfully take up the interior and exterior practices of this devotion, which I will denote in what follows, here is what you can expect:

By the light of the Holy Spirit, which He will give you through Mary, His dear Spouse, you will come to know your evil foundation, your corruption and your incapacity to do any good at all if God is not the source of it, being Himself the author of nature and of grace; and as a result of this self-knowledge you will despise yourself, you will not think of yourself except with horror. You will see yourself as a snail that spoils everything with its slime, or as a toad that poisons everything with its venom, or as a malicious serpent that desires only to deceive. Finally, the humble Mary will share with you her profound humility, which will make you despise yourself and no one else, and have a love for contempt.

The Holy Virgin will share with you her faith, which was much greater on Earth than the faith of all the patriarchs, the prophets, the apostles and all the saints. Now that she is reigning in Heaven, she no longer has this faith, because she sees everything clearly in God, by the light of glory; however, with the consent of the Most High, she did not lose it upon entering glory; she retained it in order to preserve it in the Church Militant for her most faithful servants. The more, then, that you win the favor of this august Princess and faithful Virgin, the more you will be motivated by pure faith in all your actions: a pure faith, which will free you from being anxious about things material and things extraordinary;

a lively faith animated by charity, which will make pure love the motivation for all your actions; a faith firm and unshakeable like a rock, which will make you stand firm and constant in the midst of storms and torments; an active and penetrating faith, which, like a mysterious master key, will give you access to all the mysteries of Jesus Christ, to the last things for which Man is destined, and to the very heart of God; a courageous faith, which will make you undertake and see to completion great things for God and the salvation of souls, without hesitation; finally, a faith that will be your flaming torch, your divine life, your hidden treasure of divine Wisdom, an all-powerful weapon that you will use to illuminate those who are timid and who have need of the burning gold of love, to give life to those who are dead in sin, to move and upset, by your sweet and powerful words, the hearts of stone and the cedars of Lebanon, and finally to resist the devil and all the enemies of salvation.

This beloved Mother will remove from your heart all scruples and all disordered servile fear; she will open it up and enlarge it to flow freely with the commandments of her Son, with the holy freedom of the children of God, and to introduce there the pure love of which she is the Treasury; so that you no longer behave, as you once did, out of fear of the God of love, but instead out of pure love. You will look upon Him as your good Father, whom you try to please incessantly, and with whom you converse confidently, like a child with his good father. If you have the misfortune of offending Him, you will quickly humble yourself before Him, you will humbly ask for His pardon, you will simply take His hand and lovingly get back up, without uneasiness and without anxiety, and you will continue on your journey towards Him without discouragement.

The Holy Virgin will fill you with a great confidence in God and in herself: because you will no longer approach Jesus Christ on your own, but always through this good Mother; because, having given to her all your merits, graces and satisfactions, so that she can distribute them as she wishes, she communicates to you her virtues, and clothes you with her merits, so that you can say to God with confidence: Behold Your servant Mary: let it be done to me according to Your Word: *Ecce ancilla Domini, fiat mihi secundum verbum tuum*; because, having given yourself to her completely, body and soul, she who is generous with those who are generous, and more generous than anyone, will give herself to you in return in a truly marvelous manner; in such a way that you will be able to boldly say: *Tuus sum ego, salvam me fac*: I am yours, Holy Virgin, save me; or, as I have already said, with the Beloved Disciple: *Accepi te in mea*: I have taken you, Holy Mother, as my own.

You will also be able to say, with St. Bonaventure: *Ecce Domina salvatrix mea, fiducialiter agam, et non timebo, quia fortitudo mea, et laus mea in Domino es tu...*; and in another place: *Tuus totus ego sum, et omnia mea tua sunt, o Virgo gloriosa, super omnia benedicta; ponam te ut signaculum super cor meum, quia fortis est ut mors dilectio tua (S. Bon. In psal. Min. B. V.)*: My dear Mistress and Savior, I act with confidence and I fear nothing, because you are my strength and my praise in the Lord... I am totally yours, and all that I have belongs to you; O glorious Virgin, blessed above all creation, may you be a seal upon my heart, because your love is stronger than death!

You will be able to say to God, following the sentiments of the Prophet: *Domine, non est exaltatum cor meum, neque elati sunt oculi mei; neque amulavi in magnis, neque in mirabilibus super me; si non humiliter sentiebam, sed exaltavi animam; sicut ablactatus super matre sua, ita retributio in anima mea*: Lord, neither my heart, nor my eyes have any reason to boast or to be proud, nor to search great and marvelous things; and with this, I am not yet humble, but my soul is lifted up and encouraged by confidence; I am like a child weaned away from the pleasures of the Earth and leaning on my mother's breast; and it is at this breast that I am filled with every good thing.

That which increases even more your confidence in her, is that having given her on deposit all that you have that is good, for her to give or to keep, you will have less confidence in yourself and much more in her, who is your Treasury. Oh! what confidence and what consolation for a soul who can say that the Treasury of God, wherein He has placed all He has that is most precious, is his also! *Ipsa est thesaurus Domini*: She is, says a saint, the Treasury of the Lord.

The soul of the Holy Virgin communicates itself to you for the glory of the Lord; her spirit replaces your own in order to rejoice in God, her Savior, provided that you faithfully take up the practices of this devotion. *Sit in singulis anima Mariae ut magnificet Dominum; sit in singulis spiritus Mariae, ut exultet in Deo (S. Amb.)*: May the soul of Mary be in everyone, there to glorify the Lord; may the spirit of Mary be in everyone, there to rejoice in God. Ah! when will this happy time come about, said a holy man of our day who was totally lost in Mary, ah! when will this happy time come about when the divine Mary will be established as mistress and ruler of hearts, to subjugate them fully to the empire of her great and only Son Jesus? When will souls breathe Mary as much as bodies breathe the air? At that time, marvelous things will take place in these lowly places, when the Holy Spirit, finding his dear Spouse as if reproduced in souls, will become abundantly present in them, and will fill them with His gifts, particularly His gift of wisdom, in order there to work marvels of grace. My dear brother, when will this happy time come about, this Marian era, when many souls, chosen and obtained for the Most High by Mary, losing themselves in the abyss of her interior, become living copies of Mary, to love and glorify Jesus Christ? This time will not come about until the devotion I teach is known and practiced: *Ut adveniat regnum tuum, adveniat regnum Mariae* [May the reign of Mary come, so that Your reign may come].

If Mary, who is the tree of life, is well cultivated in your soul by your faithful practice of this devotion, she will bear her fruit in good season; and her fruit is none other than Jesus Christ. I see so many devoted people who are searching for Jesus Christ, some by one way and practice, others by another; and often, after they have worked hard during the night, they can say: *Per totam noctem laborantes, nihil cepimus*: Although we have worked all night, we have caught nothing. And one could say to them: *Laborastis multum, et intulistis parum*: You have worked hard, and you have earned little; Jesus Christ is still weak within you. But by the Immaculate Way of Mary, and this divine practice which I am teaching, one works during the day, one works in a holy place, one works but a little. There is no night in Mary, because never in her was there even the slightest shadow of sin. Mary is a holy place, and the Holy of Holies, where saints are formed and molded. Take note, if you will, that I say that the saints are molded in Mary. There is a great difference between making a figure in relief, with blows of hammer and chisel, and making a figure by casting it in a mold: sculptors and statue makers work very hard to make figures in the first manner, and it takes a very long time: but to make them in the second manner, they work but a little and make them in a very short time. St. Augustine calls the Holy Virgin *forma Dei*: the mold of God: *Si forman Dei te appellem, digna existis*, the worthy mold to form and mold gods. He who is cast into this divine mold is soon formed and molded in Jesus Christ, and Jesus Christ in him: with little effort and in a short time, he will become a god, because he is cast in the same mold which formed a God.

It seems to me that I can make a good comparison between these directors and devoted persons who desire to form Jesus Christ in themselves or in others through practices other than this one, to sculptors who, placing their confidence in their own knowledge, skill and artistry, give an infinite number of blows of the hammer and chisel to a hard stone, or a piece of badly polished wood, in order to make an image of Jesus Christ; and sometimes they do not succeed at expressing Jesus Christ naturally, due either to a lack of knowledge of and experience with the person of Jesus Christ, or to some poorly executed blow, which ruined the work. But as for those who embrace this secret of grace which I present to them, I compare them truthfully to founders and molders who, having found the beautiful mold of Mary, where Jesus Christ was naturally and divinely formed, without trusting in their own skill, but solely in the quality of the mold, throw themselves into and lose themselves in Mary in order to become the natural portrait of Jesus Christ.

O what a beautiful and true comparison! But who will understand it? My desire is that it will be you, my dear brother. But remember, one only pours into a mold that which is molten and liquid: that is to say, it is necessary to destroy and melt down the old Adam within you, in order to become the new one in Mary.

By this practice, faithfully observed, you give to Jesus Christ more glory in one month's time than by any other, no matter how difficult, in several years. Here are the reasons for this: doing all your actions through the Holy Virgin, as this practice teaches, you leave behind your own intentions and operations, even though they may be good and well known to you, in order to lose yourself, in a manner of speaking, in those of the Most Holy Virgin, even though they may be unknown to you; and by this you enter into a participation in the sublime nature of her intentions, which are so pure, that she gave more glory to God by the most insignificant of her actions, for example in spinning her distaff or doing one stitch with a needle, than did St. Lawrence through his cruel martyrdom on the grill, and even more than all the saints by their most heroic actions. This had the effect that, during her sojourn here below, she attained such ineffable heights in her acquiring of graces and merits, that one could more readily count the stars in the firmament, the drops of water in the ocean and the grains of sand on the shore, than her merits and graces, and that she gave more glory to God than all the angels and saints have given Him or will give Him. O marvelous Mary! you are incapable of doing anything but marvels of grace in those souls who desire to lose themselves in you.

Because a soul, by this practice, counting as nothing all that he thinks or does on his own, and not placing his trust or taking pleasure in anything except Mary's dispositions in approaching Jesus Christ and even in speaking to Him, practices much more humility than the souls who act on their own, and who imperceptibly trust and take pleasure in their own dispositions; and, as a consequence, more exaltedly glorifies God, who is only perfectly glorified by the humble and contrite of heart.

Because the Holy Virgin, desiring, in her great charity, to receive into her virginal hands the gift of our actions, imparts to them a wonderful beauty and brilliance; she offers them herself to Jesus Christ, and without difficulty, and Our Lord is more glorified in this than if we were to offer them with our own criminal hands.

Finally, because every time you think of Mary, she, in your stead, thinks of God; every time you praise and honor Mary, she praises and honors God with you. Mary is completely relative to God, and I could rightfully call her the relation of God, who is nothing except that which she is in relation to God, or the echo of God, who neither says nor repeats anything except God. St. Elizabeth praised Mary and called her blessed because she had believed; Mary, the faithful echo of God, intoned: *Magnificat anima mea Dominum*: My soul glorifies the Lord. That which Mary did on this occasion, she does each and every day; when one praises her, loves her, honors her or gives to her, God is praised, God is loved, God is honored, God receives through Mary and in Mary.

Chapter 9

Exterior Practices

Although the essential aspect of this devotion is interior, this does not prevent it from having several exterior practices which should not be neglected: *Hæc opotuit facere et illa non omittere* [one must practice this without omitting that], either because exterior practices done well assist the interior ones, or because they remind man, who is always guided by his senses, of what he ought to do; or because they are proper for edifying one's neighbor who sees them, which those that are purely interior do not do. Let neither the worldly, nor the critical, put their nose in the air to say that true devotion is in the heart, that one must avoid that which is exterior, that therein lies the potential for vanity, that one must hide one's devotion, etc. I respond to them together with my Master: Let men see your good works, so that they may glorify your Father who is in Heaven; not, as St. Gregory says, that one should do one's actions and exterior devotions to please others and to elicit some form of praise, for that would be vanity; but one does them from time to time in front of others, with the intention of pleasing God and of glorifying Him, without worrying about the praises of men.

I will now briefly describe several exterior practices, which I call exterior, not because one does them without any interior aspect, but because they have an exterior aspect, which distinguishes them from those which are purely interior.

Preparation for Consecration

Those who would like to enter into this particular devotion (which has not yet been set up as a confraternity, although that is the goal), after having taken at least twelve days to empty themselves of the spirit of this world, which is contrary to that of Jesus Christ, should take three weeks to fill themselves with Jesus Christ through the Most Holy Virgin. Here is the plan they should follow:

During the first week, they will direct all their prayers and pious acts to asking for knowledge of themselves and contrition for their sins; and they should do everything in the spirit of humility. To this end, they can, if they desire, meditate on what I have said about our evil foundation, and regard themselves during this week as nothing more than snails, slugs, toads, pigs, serpents and goats; or meditate on these three words of St. Bernard: *Cogita quid fueris, semen putridum; quid sis vas stercorum; quid futurus sis, esca vermium* [think of that which you were, a piece of mud; of that which you are, a wisp of smoke; of that which you will be, the food of worms]. They will pray by these words to ask Our Lord and His Holy Spirit to enlighten them: *Domine ut videam* [Lord that I might see]; or *Noverim me* [that I might know myself]; or *Veni, Sancte Spiritus* [Come Holy Spirit], and should say every day the Litanies of the Holy Spirit [see Appendix] and the prayer that follows, as noted in the first pages of this work [refers to lost pages of the manuscript]. They will have recourse to the Most Holy Virgin, and ask her for this great grace [of knowing themselves and their sins], which ought to be the foundation of all the others, and to this end they will say every day the *Ave maris Stella*, and her Litanies [see Appendix].

During the second week, they will apply themselves in all their prayers and works each day to knowing the Most Holy Virgin. They will ask this knowledge of the Holy Spirit. They can read and meditate on that which we have said about her. They will recite, as during the first week, the Litanies of the Holy Spirit and the *Ave maris Stella* [see Appendix], and in addition, a complete Rosary every day, or at least a third of the Rosary, for this intention.

They will use the third week to know Jesus Christ. They can read and meditate on that which we have said about Him, and say the prayer of St. Augustine, which is found toward the beginning of this second part [see Chapter 3]. They can, with the same saint, say and repeat hundreds of times each day: *Noverim te*: Lord, that I might know You! Or *Domine, ut videam*: Lord, that I might see You for who You are! They will recite, as in the preceding weeks, the Litanies of the Holy Spirit and the *Ave maris Stella*, and add each day the Litanies of Jesus [see Appendix].

At the end of these three weeks, they will go to Confession and Communion with the intention of giving themselves to Jesus Christ as slaves of love, through the hands of Mary. And, after Communion, which they will try to make following the method which is described in what follows [see Chapter 11], they will recite the prayer of consecration, which is also found in what follows [see Appendix]; they should write it out, or have it written for them if it is not already printed, and they should sign it the on same day. It would also be good if, on this day, they were to pay some tribute to Jesus Christ and His Holy Mother, either out of penance for their past infidelity to the vows of their Baptism, or in order to manifest their subordination to the reign of Jesus and Mary. This tribute should be according to the devotion and capacity of each person; such as a fast, a mortification, an alms, or a candle; even if they give only a pin in homage, but with a good heart, it is enough for Jesus, who looks only at the good intention.

At least every year, on the same date, they will renew the same consecration, observing the same practices for three weeks.

They can even, every month or every day, renew all that they have done, by these few words: *Tuus totus ego sum, et omnia mea tua sunt*: I am all Yours, and all that I have belongs to You, O my dear Jesus, through Mary, Your Holy Mother.

The Little Crown of the Most Holy Virgin

They will willingly recite every day of their lives, the Little
Crown of the Most Holy Virgin, composed of three *Paters* and
twelve *Aves*, in honor of the twelve privileges and grandeurs of
the Most Holy Virgin. This practice is very ancient and has its
foundation in Holy Scripture. St. John saw a woman crowned
with twelve stars, clothed with the sun, and holding the moon
beneath her feet; this woman is, according to interpreters, the
Most Holy Virgin. There are several good ways of reciting it,
which would take too long to describe; the Holy Spirit will
teach them to those who are the most faithful to this devotion.
However, to recite it in its simplest form, one should start by
saying: *Dignare me laudare te, Virgo sacrata; da mihi virtutem
contra hostes tuos* [Deign to hear me when I praise you, O
Holy Virgin, and give me strength against your enemies]; then,
one says the *Credo*, then a *Pater*, then four *Aves* and a *Gloria
Patri*; and so on for the remainder. At the end, one says: *Sub
tuum præsidium* [First words of the prayer: We have recourse
to your protection, Holy Mother of God. Reject not the prayers
we address to you in our need, but deliver us always from all
danger, O glorious and blessed Virgin].

Little Chains

It is most praiseworthy and glorious and beneficial to those who
have thus made themselves slaves of Jesus in Mary, to wear, as
a sign of their loving slavery, little chains of iron that have been
blessed by an appropriate blessing. These exterior signs are, in
truth, not essential, and a person, even though he has embraced
this devotion, could very well do without them; however, I
cannot help but praise those who, after having shaken off the
shameful chains of slavery to the devil, in which Original Sin
and possibly actual sins had held them, have voluntarily entered
into the glorious slavery of Jesus Christ, and boast together with

St. Paul about being in chains for Jesus Christ, chains that are a thousand times more glorious and precious, even though of iron and without brilliance, than all the gold necklaces of the emperors.

Even though in former days there was nothing more infamous than the cross, at present this wood is unceasingly the most glorious object in Christianity. Let us say the same for the irons of slavery. There is nothing more ignominious among the ancients, and even today among the pagans; but, among the Christians, there is nothing more illustrious than the chains of Jesus Christ, because they deliver us and keep us from the infamous bonds of sin and of the devil; because they set us free, and bind us to Jesus and Mary, not by constraint and force, like those sentenced to forced labor, but by charity and love, like children: *Traham eos in vinculis charitatis (Hosea 11:4)*: I will draw them to myself, says God through the mouth of a prophet, by chains of charity, which are, therefore, as strong as death, and in a way even stronger for those who are faithful at wearing these glorious signs until death. Because, although death destroys their body by corruption, it will never destroy the bonds of their slavery, which, being made of iron, are not easily corrupted; and perhaps, on the day of the resurrection of the body, at the great Last Judgment, these chains, which will still bind their bones, will become a part of their glory, and will be changed into chains of light and glory. A thousand times happy the illustrious slaves of Jesus in Mary, who wear their chains to the grave! Here are the reasons for wearing these little chains:

First, it is to remind the Christian of the vows and promises of his Baptism, of the perfect renewal he made by this devotion, and of the strict obligation he is under to be faithful to it. Knowing that man, who is so often guided more by his senses than by pure faith, forgets easily his obligations to God if there is nothing external to remind him of them, these little chains serve marvelously to remind the Christian of the chains of sin and of the slavery to the devil from which Holy Baptism delivered him, and of the dependence on Jesus Christ that he vowed in Holy Baptism, and of the ratification of this that he made in the renewal of his vows; and one of the reasons so few Christians think of their baptismal vows, and then live with license like the pagans, as if they had never promised anything to God, is that they do not wear any exterior sign as a reminder to themselves.

Secondly, it is to show that one is not at all embarrassed by slavery and servitude to Jesus Christ, and that one renounces the deadly slavery to the world, to sin, and to the devil.

Thirdly, it is to protect and preserve oneself from the chains of sin and the devil. For one must wear either the chains of iniquity, or the chains of charity and salvation: *Vincula peccatorum; in vinculis charitatis.*

Ah! My dear brother, let us break the chains of sin and sinners, of the world and the worldly, of the devil and his henchmen, and let us resoundingly reject their deadly yoke: *Dirumpamus vincula eorum et projiciamus a nobis jugum ipsorum*: Let us place our feet, to use an expression of the Holy Spirit, into His glorious fetters, and our necks into His collars: *Injice pedem tuum in compedes illius, et in torques illius collum tuum (Eccl. 6:24)*: Let us submit our shoulders, and take up Wisdom, who is Jesus Christ, and let us not be bothered by these chains: *Subjice humerum tuum et porta illam, et ne acedieris vinculis ejus (Eccl. 6:25)*. Note that the Holy Spirit, before saying these words, prepares the soul for them, in order that the soul does not reject His important counsels; these are the words: *Audi, fili, et accipe consilium intellectus, et ne abjicias consolium meum (Eccl. 6:23)*: Listen, my son, and receive a counsel of understanding, and do not reject my counsels.

Allow me, my very dear friend, to join with the Holy Spirit and give you the same advice: *Vincula illius alligatura salutis (Eccl. 6:29)*: these chains are chains of salvation. Since Jesus Christ on the cross must draw all men to Himself, whether they desire it or not, He will draw the damned by the chains of their sins, to chain them up like forced laborers and devils to His eternal ire and his vengeful justice: but He will draw, particularly in these last days, the predestined by chains of charity: *Omnia traham ad meipsum. Traham eos in vinculis charitatis (Hosea 11:4)*.

These loving slaves of Jesus Christ, or enchained of Jesus Christ, *vincti Christi*, can wear their chains either around their neck, or on their arm, or around their waist, or on their feet. Fr. Vincent Caraffa, seventh general of the Company of Jesus, who died in the odor of sanctity in the year 1643, wore, as a sign of his servitude, a circle of iron on his feet, and said that his only pain was that he could not wear his chain out in the open. Mother Agnes of Jesus, of whom we have spoken, wore a chain of iron around her waist. Several others have worn them around their necks, as penance for the necklaces of pearls they once wore in the world. Several others wore them on their arms, in order to remind themselves, while working with their hands, that they are slaves of Jesus Christ.

The Mystery of the Incarnation

They will have a singular devotion to the great Mystery of the Incarnation of the Word, the 25th of March, which is the proper Mystery of this devotion, since this devotion was inspired by the Holy Spirit: to honor and imitate the ineffable dependence that God the Son desired to have upon Mary, for the glory of God the Father and for their salvation, a dependence which shows itself in a particular way in this Mystery where Jesus Christ is captive and slave in the womb of the divine Mary, and where He depends on her for everything; to give thanks to God for the incomparable graces He gave to Mary and particularly the fact that He chose her to be His worthy Mother, a choice that was made in this Mystery: these are the two principal ends of slavery to Jesus Christ in Mary. Take note, if you will, that I say ordinarily "slave of Jesus in Mary", or "slavery of Jesus in Mary". One could, in truth, as others have done, say "slave of Mary", or "slavery of the Holy Virgin"; but I believe that it is more worthwhile to call oneself a "slave of Jesus in Mary", as Mr. Tronson, superior general of the Seminary of St. Sulpice, renowned for his rare prudence and consummate piety, had advised an ecclesiastic who consulted him on this subject. Here are the reasons for this:

Since we are in a prideful century, when there are a great number of egotistical intellectuals, strong-willed and critical, who find something to criticize in even the most well established and solid devotions, and in order to avoid giving them another unnecessary occasion to criticize, it is more worthwhile to say "slavery of Jesus Christ in Mary", and to call oneself a "slave of Jesus Christ", rather than a "slave of Mary"; taking the name of this devotion from its final goal, which is Jesus Christ, rather than the way and the means for achieving this goal, which is Mary; although one could in truth do one or the other without scruple, as I myself have done. For example, a man who is going from Orleans to Tours, by way of Amboise, could very well say that he is going to Amboise or that he is going to Tours; that he is a traveler to Amboise or a traveler to Tours; with this difference, however, that Amboise is but the direct route to go to Tours, and that Tours alone is his final goal and the destination of his journey.

Since the principal Mystery one celebrates and honors in this devotion is the Mystery of the Incarnation, wherein one cannot see Jesus except in Mary and incarnate in her womb, it is more appropriate to say "slavery of Jesus in Mary", or "slavery of

Jesus residing and reigning in Mary", following this beautiful prayer said by so many great men: O Jesus, living in Mary, come and live in us, in your spirit of holiness, etc.

This manner of speaking shows better the union that exists between Jesus and Mary. They are so intimately united, that one is all in the other; Jesus is all in Mary, and Mary is all in Jesus; or more exactly, she is no more, but Jesus alone in her; and one could more readily separate the light from the sun than Mary from Jesus. All this means that one could call Our Lord "Jesus of Mary", and the Holy Virgin "Mary of Jesus".

Time does not permit me to stop here to explain the wonders and the grandeurs of Jesus living and reigning in Mary, or of the Incarnation of the Word, so I will content myself with saying in three words that this is the first Mystery of Jesus Christ, the most hidden, the most elevated and the least known; that it is in this Mystery that Jesus, in concert with Mary, in her womb, which is for this reason called by the saints *aula sacramentorum*, the room of the secrets of God, chose all the elect; that it is in this Mystery that He worked all the mysteries of His life which followed, by the acceptance He had offered: *Jesus ingrediens mundum dicit: Ecce venio ut faciam, voluntatem tuam, etc.*; and, as a consequence, that this Mystery is a summary of all the mysteries, which encompasses the will and the grace of all of them; finally, that this Mystery is the Throne of the mercy, the generosity and the glory of God. The throne of His mercy towards us, because, since one cannot approach Jesus nor speak to Him except through Mary, one cannot see Jesus nor talk to Him except by the mediation of Mary. Jesus, who always grants the prayers of His dear Mother, thereby always grants His grace and His mercy to poor sinners: *Adeamus ergo cum fiducia ad thronum gratiæ.* It is the throne of His generosity for Mary, because during the time this new Adam dwelled in this true terrestrial Paradise, He worked there so many marvels in secret, that neither the angels nor men understand them at all; this is why the saints call Mary the Magnificence of God: *Magnificentia Dei*, as if God were not magnificent except in Mary: *Solummodo ibi magnificus est Dominus*. It is the throne of His glory for His Father, because it was in Mary that Jesus Christ perfectly appeased His Father, who was angry at humanity; in Mary He perfectly restored the glory, which sin had ravaged; and, by the sacrifice He made of His will and of Himself, He gave more glory to Him than had ever been given Him by all the sacrifices of the Old Law, and finally, in this He gave Him infinite glory, which He had never before received from a Man.

The *Ave Maria*

They will have a great devotion to reciting the *Ave Maria*, or the Angelic Salutation, of which few Christians, however enlightened, know the value, the merit, the excellence and the necessity. It was necessary that the Holy Virgin appear several times to great saints who were well enlightened in order to show them the merit of it, as to St. Dominic, St. John of Capistrano, and Blessed Alan de la Roche. They composed entire books about the marvels and the efficacy of this prayer for the conversion of souls; they openly publicized and publicly preached: that since the salvation of the world was begun by means of the *Ave Maria*, the salvation of each individual is therefore attached to this prayer; and that since this prayer caused the Fruit of Life to come to the dry and sterile earth, this same prayer, when well said, will cause the Word of God to grow in our souls and to bear the Fruit of Life, Jesus Christ; they proclaimed that the *Ave Maria* is a heavenly dew which waters the earth, that is, the soul, to cause it to bring forth fruit in due time, and that a soul not watered by this prayer or heavenly dew does not bring forth any fruit at all, and produces nothing but brambles and thorns, and is ready to be cursed.

Here then is what the Most Holy Virgin revealed to Blessed Alan de la Roche, as he remarks in his book *De dignitate Rosarii* [On the Dignity of the Rosary], and also through Cartagena: Know this, my son, and make it known to everyone, that a probable and immediate sign of eternal damnation is when one has an aversion for, is indifferent to and is negligent towards saying the Angelic Salutation, which renewed all of humanity: *Scias enim et secure intelligas et inde late omnibus patefacias, quod videlicet signum probabile est et propinquum æternæ damnationis horrere et attediari ac negligere Salutationem angelicam, totius mundi reparativam (Lib. de Dignit. Cap. II).* These are words both consoling and terrifying, and one would have a hard time believing them if we did not have the word of this holy man, and St. Dominic before him, as well as other great persons after them, and the experience of several centuries. Because it has always been noted that those who carry the mark of damnation, such as the heretics and the impious, the proud and the worldly, truly hate or despise the *Ave Maria* and the Rosary. The heretics learn and still recite the *Pater*, but not the *Ave Maria*, nor the Rosary; it is their horror; they would sooner wear a serpent around them than a Rosary. The proud also, even Catholics, having the same inclinations as their father Lucifer, despise or have nothing but indifference for the *Ave Maria*, and regard the Rosary as a devotion for the weak, and good only for the ignorant and the illiterate. To the contrary, we have seen by experience that those who have other great marks of predestination love, savor and recite with pleasure the *Ave Maria*; and the more they belong to God, the more they love this prayer. This is what the Holy Virgin said also to Blessed Alan, after those words I quoted above.

I do not know how or why this is so, but it is nevertheless true; and I have no better secret for knowing whether or not a person is of God, than to determine if he loves to say the *Ave Maria* and the Rosary. I say "he loves"; because it can happen that a person has a natural incapacity or supernatural incapacity to say it, but he loves it all the same, and inspires others to love it as well.

You predestined souls, you slaves of Jesus in Mary, learn well that the *Ave Maria* is the most beautiful of all prayers after the *Pater*; it is the most perfect compliment you can offer to Mary, since it is the compliment which the Most High sent to her by an archangel in order to win her heart; and it was so powerful over her heart, by the secret charms of which it is full, that Mary gave her consent to the Incarnation of the Word, in spite of her profound humility. And it is by this compliment that you also will unfailingly win her heart, if you say it as it should be said.

The *Ave Maria* said well, that is to say, with attention, devotion and modesty, is, according to the saints, the enemy of the devil, which puts him to flight, and the hammer that crushes him, the sanctification of the soul, the joy of angels, the melody of the predestined, the Canticle of the New Testament, the pleasure of Mary and the glory of the Most Holy Trinity. The *Ave Maria* is a heavenly dew that renders fruitful the soul, it is a chaste and loving kiss that one gives to Mary, it is a vermillion rose that one presents to her, it is a precious pearl that one offers to her, it is a touch of ambrosia and nectar that one gives to her. All of these comparisons come from the saints.

I urgently beg you, because of the love you carry for Jesus and Mary, not to be content with reciting the Little Crown of the Holy Virgin, but also the Rosary (five decades), and even, if you have the time for it, the entire Rosary (fifteen decades) every day, and you will bless, at the hour of your death, the day and the hour when you believed me; and after having sown the blessings of Jesus and Mary, you will reap eternal blessings in Heaven: *Qui seminat in benedictionibus, de benedictionibus et metet.*

The *Magnificat*

To thank God for the graces He gave to the Most Holy Virgin, they will say the *Magnificat* often, following the example of

Blessed Marie d'Oignies and of many other saints. It is the only prayer and the only work composed by the Holy Virgin, or rather composed by Jesus through her, for He spoke through her mouth. It is the greatest sacrifice of praise that God has received in the law of grace. It is on the one hand the most humble and the most thankful, and on the other hand the most sublime and the most elevated of all the canticles: there are mysteries in this canticle so great and so hidden that the angels do not know them. Gerson, who was a very pious and learned doctor, after having spent a great part of his life in composing treatises full of erudition and piety about the most difficult of subjects, did not undertake to explain the *Magnificat*, except with trembling and at the end of his life, as the crowning achievement of his works. He recounts, in a tract he composed about it, many wonderful things about this beautiful and divine canticle. Among others, he says that the Most Holy Virgin herself recited it often, particularly after Holy Communion, as an act of thanksgiving. The learned Benzonius, in explaining this same *Magnificat*, recounts several miracles resulting from its virtue, and says that the demons tremble and take flight when they hear these words of the *Magnificat*: *Fecit potentiem in brachio suo, dispersit superbos mente cordis sui* [He has shown forth the strength of His arm, He has scattered the proud in their conceit].

Chapter 10

Interior Practices

Beyond the exterior practices of this devotion which we have just listed, which one should not omit either by negligence or by contempt as far as each person's state and condition of life permits, there are the following interior practices which are most sanctifying for those whom the Holy Spirit calls to a high degree of perfection:

In four words, one must do everything through Mary, with Mary, in Mary, and for Mary, in order to do everything more perfectly through Jesus, with Jesus, in Jesus and for Jesus.

Through Mary

One should do everything through Mary, that is to say, one should obey the Most Holy Virgin in everything, and be led in every way by her spirit, which is the Holy Spirit of God. Those who are led by the Spirit of God are children of God: *Qui spiritu Dei aguntur, ii sunt filii Dei.* Those who are led by the spirit of Mary are children of Mary, and consequently, children of God, as we have shown, and among so many devotees of the Holy Virgin, the only true and faithful devotees are those who are led by her spirit. I said that the spirit of Mary is the Spirit of God, because she was never led by her own spirit, but always by the Spirit of God, who became so much her master that He became her own spirit. This is why St. Ambrose said: *Sit in singulis, etc.*: May the soul of Mary be in each one so he might glorify the Lord; may the spirit of Mary be in each one so he might rejoice in God.

How happy the soul who follows the example of a good Jesuit brother whose name was Rodriguez, and who died in the odor of sanctity, by fully belonging to and being guided by Mary's spirit, which is gentle and strong, zealous and prudent, humble and courageous, pure and fruitful!

In order to allow itself to be led by this spirit of Mary, the soul must renounce its own spirit, its own light and its own will before taking any action: for example, before praying, saying or hearing the Holy Mass, receiving Holy Communion, etc., because the darkness of our own spirit and the evil of our own will and plans, if we follow them, even if they appear to us to be good, are obstacles to the holy spirit of Mary. One must give oneself over to the spirit of Mary to be moved and led by her in the manner she desires. One must place oneself and abandon oneself into her virginal hands, as a tool in the hands of a worker, as a lute in the hands of a great musician. One must lose oneself and abandon oneself in her, like a stone thrown into the ocean; that which is done simply and in an instant, by a single glance of the spirit, a tiny movement of the will, or verbally in saying, for example, "I renounce myself, I give myself to you, my dear Mother"; and even though one does not sense any sweetness in this act of union, it is nevertheless real. (For if someone were to say, with enough sincerity, "I give myself to the devil", which would certainly be most displeasing God, then, even without perceiving any change in feeling, that person would nevertheless belong to the devil.) One should therefore, from time to time, during an action and after an action, renew this act of union with Mary; and the more one does this, the sooner one is sanctified, and the sooner one attains union with Jesus Christ, which is always the necessary result of union with Mary, because the spirit of Mary is the Spirit of Jesus.

With Mary

One should do one's actions with Mary: that is to say, one should, in one's actions, look to Mary as an accomplished model of every virtue and perfection, which the Holy Spirit formed in a pure creature, to imitate as much as our limited reach allows. We should, therefore, in every action, look to Mary for how she acted or how she would act if she were in our place. In order to do this, we should examine and meditate on the great virtues she practiced during her life, particularly: her lively faith, by which she believed without hesitation the words of the Angel, and by which she believed faithfully and continuously right up to the foot of the cross on Calvary; her profound humility, which made her conceal herself, remain in silence, be submissive in everything and place herself last; her totally divine purity, which never had and never will have any equal under the heavens, and finally, all her other virtues.

Let us remember, I repeat a second time, that Mary is the great and unique mold of God, fit for making living images of God, with little effort and in a short time; and that a soul which has found this mold, and loses itself in it, is quickly changed into Jesus Christ, whom this mold naturally produces.

In Mary

One should do all one's actions in Mary. In order to fully understand this practice, one must realize that the Most Holy Virgin is the true terrestrial Paradise of the New Adam, and that the former terrestrial Paradise was but a prefiguring. There are, therefore, in this terrestrial Paradise, inexplicable riches, beauties, rarities and sweetness, which the New Adam, Jesus Christ, has left there. It is here, in this Paradise, where He took pleasure in remaining for nine months, where He worked His marvels and where He laid out His riches with the magnificence of a God. This most holy place is composed entirely of virgin and immaculate earth, from which the New Adam was formed and nourished, without any stain or blemish, by the operation of the Holy Spirit who dwells there. It is here, in this terrestrial Paradise, where the true Tree of Life is found, which bore Jesus Christ, the fruit of life; the tree of the knowledge of good and evil, which provided the Light to the world. There are, in this divine place, trees planted by the hand of God and watered with His divine anointing, which have born and which daily bear fruits of divine flavor; there are flower beds dotted with beautiful and varied flowers of virtue, which give off a fragrance which perfumes even the angels. There are in this place green meadows of hope, impenetrable towers of strength, delightful houses of confidence; it is only the Holy Spirit who can make known the truth hidden under these material symbols. There is in this place the pure and uncontaminated air of chastity; a beautiful day, without night, of holy humanity; a beautiful sun, without shadow, of the Divinity; a continually burning furnace of love, where all the iron placed therein is fired and changed to gold; there is a river of humility, which gushes out of the earth and which, dividing into four branches, waters this entire enchanted place; and these branches are the four cardinal virtues.

The Holy Spirit, through the mouths of the Church Fathers, also called the Holy Virgin: the Eastern Door, through which the High Priest Jesus Christ enters and leaves the world: through her He entered the first time, and He will come this way the second time; the Sanctuary of the Divinity; the resting place of the Most Holy Trinity; the Throne of God; the City of God; the Altar of God; the Temple of God; the World of God. All these different epithets and praises are absolutely truthful, in light of the many marvels and graces the Most High brought about in Mary. Oh! what riches! Oh! what glory! Oh! what pleasure! Oh!

what happiness to be able to enter into and dwell in Mary, where the Most High has set up the throne of His supreme glory!

But it is difficult for sinners like us to have the permission and the capacity and the enlightenment to enter a place so elevated and holy, which is guarded not by a cherubim, as was the former terrestrial Paradise, but by the Holy Spirit Himself, who has made Himself the absolute master of it, of which He said: *Hortus conclusus soror mea sponsa, hortus conclusus, fons signatus.* Mary is closed; Mary is sealed; the wretched children of Adam and Eve, chased out of the earthly Paradise, are not able to enter therein except by a singular grace of the Holy Spirit, a grace they must merit.

After having obtained, by one's faithfulness, this signal grace, one must abide in the beautiful interior of Mary with pleasure, rest there in peace, rely on her with confidence, hide there in assurance, and lose oneself there without reservation, so that, in this virginal womb, the soul is nourished with the milk of her maternal grace and mercy, is delivered from its confusion, fears and scruples, is secure against all its enemies, the devil, the world and sin, which can never enter there; which is why she says that those who abide in her will never sin: *Qui operantur in me, non peccabunt*, that is to say that those who abide in the Holy Virgin in spirit will never commit grave sin; in order that the soul be formed in Jesus Christ, and Jesus Christ in the soul; because her womb is, as the Church Fathers have said, the chamber of divine Sacraments, where Jesus Christ and all the elect are formed: *Homo et homo natus est in ea* [a man and a man is born of her].

For Mary

Finally, one should do all one's actions for Mary. Having totally given oneself over to her service, it is only right that one does everything for her as a valet, a servant and a slave; not that one considers her the final goal of one's service, which is Jesus Christ alone, but as the intermediate goal and its mysterious means, and the easy way to go to Him. Thus, like a good servant and slave, one should not rest in laziness; instead, one should, supported by her protection, undertake and do great things for this august Sovereign. One should defend her privileges when they are disputed; one should support her glory when it is attacked; one should attract everyone, if one is able, to her service and to this true devotion; one should speak and cry out against those who abuse her devotion and thereby outrage her Son, and at the same time work to establish this true devotion; one should not claim any recompense from her for one's little services, except the honor of belonging to such a loveable Princess, and the happiness of being united through her to Jesus, her Son, by an indissoluble bond in time and for all eternity.

Glory to Jesus in Mary!
Glory to Mary in Jesus!
Glory to God alone!

Chapter 11

At Holy Communion

As preparation for receiving our Lord in Holy Communion, you first humble yourself profoundly before God; you renounce your own totally corrupted foundation, and your dispositions, no matter how good your self-love makes them seem; and you renew your consecration by saying: *Tuus totus ego sum, et omnia mea tua sunt*: I am all yours my dear Mistress, and all that I have belongs to you.

You ask this good Mother to prepare your heart to receive her Son with the same dispositions. You tell her that the glory of her Son is at stake by His being placed into a heart as defiled and inconstant as your own, since it could diminish His glory or cause it to be lost; but if she desires to inhabit your heart in order to receive her Son, she can do this because of the dominion she has over hearts, and her Son would be well received without stain and without danger of being outraged or lost: *Deus in medio ejus non commovebitur* [God is in her, she cannot falter]. You tell her confidently that all that you have given to her of what you have does little to honor her, but that, by Holy Communion, you desire to give her the same gift that the eternal Father gave to her, and that she will be more honored by this than if you were to give her all the wealth of the world; and finally, that Jesus, who loves her uniquely, desires to once again delight in her and rest in her, even if it is in your soul, which is dirtier and poorer than the stable into which Jesus had no trouble coming because she was there. You ask for her heart by these tender words: *Accipio te in mea omnia. Praebe mihi cor tuum, o Maria*! [I take you for my all. Give me your heart, O Mary]

After the *Pater*, ready to receive Jesus Christ, you say three times: *Domine, non sum dignus, etc.* [Lord, I am not worthy...]; it is as if the first time you are addressing the Father, and saying to Him that you are not worthy, because of your evil thoughts and lack of gratitude toward such a good Father, to receive His only Son, but here is Mary, His servant: *Ecce ancilla Domini* [here is the servant of the Lord], who will receive Him for you, and who gives you confidence and singular hope before His Majesty: *Quoniam singulariter in spe constituisti me* [You alone make me dwell in safety].

You then say to the Son: *Domine, non sum dignus*, etc., that you are not worthy to receive Him because of your useless and evil words and your infidelity in His service; however, you beseech Him to have pity on you because you will bring Him into the home of His Mother, and you will not permit Him to go without His coming to stay in her home: *Tenui eum, nec dimittam, donec introducam illum in dumum matris meae, et in cubiculum genitricis meae (Cant. 3:4)*. You beseech Him to arise and come to His resting place and to the Ark of His sanctification: *Surge, Domine, in requiem tuam, tu et arca sanctificationis tuae*. You say to Him that you no longer place your confidence in your own merits, your own strength or your own preparations, as did Esau, but in those of Mary, your dear Mother, as did little Jacob as he was cared for by Rebecca; that, despite the sinner and the Esau that you are, you dare to approach His Holiness supported by and adorned with the merits and virtues of His Holy Mother.

You then say to the Holy Spirit: *Domine, non sum dignus*, etc., that you are not worthy to receive the Masterpiece of His love, because of the tepidness and the sinfulness of your actions and because of your resistance to His inspirations, but that all your confidence is in Mary, His faithful Spouse; and you say with St. Bernard: *Haec maxima mea fiducia; haec tota ratio spei meae* [she is my great security; she is my reason for hope]. You can even beseech Him to descend once again into Mary, His inseparable Spouse; that Her womb is as pure and her heart is as on fire as ever before; and that without His descending into your soul, neither Jesus nor Mary will be formed there, nor will they find worthy lodging there.

After Holy Communion, having collected your thoughts, and with eyes closed, you introduce Jesus Christ into the heart of Mary. You give Him to His Mother, who receives Him lovingly, places Him honorably, adores Him profoundly, loves Him perfectly, embraces Him tightly, and renders to Him, in spirit and in truth, many services that are unknown to us in our dense interior darkness.

Or you may remain profoundly humbled in your heart, in the presence of Jesus living in Mary. Or you can wait as a slave waits at the door of the King's palace, where He is speaking with the Queen; and while they are speaking to each other, with no need of you, you go in your mind throughout Heaven and Earth, beseeching all creatures to thank, adore and love Jesus and Mary in your place: *Venite, adoremus, venite,* etc. [Come, let us adore, come,...].

Or you yourself may ask Jesus, in union with Mary, for the coming of His Kingdom on Earth through His Holy Mother, or for divine wisdom, or for divine love, or for the pardon of your sins, or some other grace, but always through Mary and in Mary: saying with self-deprecation: *Ne respicias, Domine, peccata me:* Lord, look not upon my sins; *sed oculi tui videant aequitates Mariae*: but that your eyes may see in me only the virtues and the merits of Mary. And, in calling to mind your sins, you may add: *Inimicus homo hoc fecit*: The burden I carry is that I am my own greatest enemy; I myself have committed these sins; or *Ab homine iniquo et doloso erue me,* or *Te oportet crescere, me autem minui*: My Jesus, You must increase in my soul, and I must decrease. Mary, you must increase within me, and I must become less than ever. *Crescite et multiplicamini*: O Jesus and Mary, increase in me, and multiply in others.

There are an infinite number of other thoughts that the Holy Spirit provides, and will provide to you if you are interior, mortified and faithful to this great and sublime devotion which I have just taught to you. But remember that the more you allow Mary to act in your Communion, the more Jesus will be glorified; the more you profoundly humble yourself, the more you will allow Mary to act through Jesus, and Jesus in Mary; and finally, listen to them, in peace and in silence, without making any effort to see, taste or feel; because the just live everywhere by faith, and especially at Holy Communion, which is an act of faith: *Justus meus ex fide vivit* [My just ones live by faith].

Appendix

Prayers

The following prayers are not part of the original manuscript, but are included here to facilitate preparing for and making the act of consecration to Jesus through Mary.

Litany of the Holy Spirit

Lord, have mercy on us,
Christ have mercy on us.
Lord, have mercy on us.

Father all powerful, *Have mercy on us.*
Jesus, Eternal Son of the Father, Redeemer of the world,
Save us.
Spirit of the Father and the Son, boundless Life of both,
Sanctify us.

Holy Trinity, *Hear us.*
Holy Spirit, Who proceedest from the Father and the Son,
Enter our hearts.
Holy Spirit, Who art equal to the Father and the Son,
Enter our hearts.

Promise of God the Father, *Have mercy on us.*
Ray of heavenly light, *Have mercy on us.*
Author of all good, *Have mercy on us.*
Source of heavenly water, *Have mercy on us.*
Consuming Fire, *Have mercy on us.*

Ardent Charity, *Have mercy on us.*
Spiritual Unction, *Have mercy on us.*
Spirit of love and truth, *Have mercy on us.*
Spirit of wisdom and understanding, *Have mercy on us.*
Spirit of counsel and fortitude, *Have mercy on us.*
Spirit of knowledge and piety, *Have mercy on us.*
Spirit of the fear of the Lord, *Have mercy on us.*
Spirit of grace and prayer, *Have mercy on us.*
Spirit of peace and meekness, *Have mercy on us.*
Spirit of modesty and innocence, *Have mercy on us.*
Holy Spirit, the Comforter, *Have mercy on us.*
Holy Spirit, the Sanctifier, *Have mercy on us.*
Holy Spirit, Who governest the Church, *Have mercy on us.*
Gift of God the Most High, *Have mercy on us.*
Spirit Who fillest the universe, *Have mercy on us.*
Spirit of the adoption of the children of God,
Have mercy on us.
Holy Spirit, *Inspire us with horror of sin.*
Holy Spirit, *Come and renew the face of the earth.*
Holy Spirit, *Shed Thy Light into our souls.*
Holy Spirit, *Engrave Thy law in our hearts.*
Holy Spirit, *Inflame us with the flame of Thy love.*
Holy Spirit, *Open to us the treasures of Thy graces.*
Holy Spirit, *Teach us to pray well.*
Holy Spirit, *Enlighten us with Thy heavenly inspirations.*
Holy Spirit, *Lead us in the way of salvation.*
Holy Spirit, *Grant us the only necessary knowledge.*
Holy Spirit, *Inspire in us the practice of good.*
Holy Spirit, *Grant us the merits of all virtues.*
Holy Spirit, *Make us persevere in justice.*
Holy Spirit, *Be our everlasting reward.*

Lamb of God, Who takest away the sins of the world,
Send us Thy Holy Spirit.
Lamb of God, Who takest away the sins of the world,

Pour down into our souls the gifts of the Holy Spirit.
Lamb of God, Who takest away the sins of the world,
Grant us the Spirit of wisdom and piety.

Come, Holy Spirit! Fill the hearts of Thy faithful,
And enkindle in them the fire of Thy love.

Let Us Pray: Grant, O merciful Father, that Thy Divine Spirit
may enlighten, inflame and purify us, that He may penetrate
us with His heavenly dew and make us fruitful in good works,
through Our Lord Jesus Christ, Thy Son, Who with Thee, in the
unity of the same Spirit, liveth and reigneth forever and ever.
Amen.

Ave Maris Stella

Hail thou star of ocean
Portal of the sky
Ever virgin Mother
Of the Lord Most High

O! by Gabriel's Ave
Uttered long ago,
Eva's name reversing,
Established peace below

Break the captives' fetters,
Light on blindness pour,
All our ills expelling,
Every bliss implore

Show thyself a Mother,
Offer Him our sighs,
Who for us incarnate
Did not thee despise
Virgin of all virgins
To thy shelter take us,
Gentlest of the gentle
Chaste and gentle make us

Still, as on we journey,
Help our weak endeavor,
Till with thee and Jesus
We rejoice forever
Through the highest Heaven,
To the almighty Three
Father, Son, and Spirit,
One same glory be.

Amen.

Litany of the Blessed Virgin Mary

Lord, have mercy on us.
Christ, have mercy on us.
Lord, have mercy on us.

Christ, hear us. *Christ, graciously hear us.*

God the Father of heaven, *Have mercy on us.*
God the Son, Redeemer of the world, *Have mercy on us.*
God the Holy Ghost, *Have mercy on us.*

Holy Trinity, one God, *Have mercy on us.*
Holy Mary, *Pray for us.*
Holy Mother of God, *Pray for us.*
Holy Virgin of virgins, *Pray for us.*
Mother of Christ, *Pray for us.*
Mother of divine grace, *Pray for us.*
Mother most pure, *Pray for us.*
Mother most chaste, *Pray for us.*
Mother inviolate, *Pray for us.*
Mother undefiled, *Pray for us.*
Mother most amiable, *Pray for us.*
Mother most admirable, *Pray for us.*
Mother of good counsel, *Pray for us.*
Mother of our Creator, *Pray for us.*
Mother of our Savior, *Pray for us.*
Virgin most prudent, *Pray for us.*
Virgin most venerable, *Pray for us.*
Virgin most renowned, *Pray for us.*
Virgin most powerful, *Pray for us.*
Virgin most merciful, *Pray for us.*
Virgin most faithful, *Pray for us.*
Mirror of justice, *Pray for us.*
Seat of wisdom, *Pray for us.*

Cause of our joy, *Pray for us.*
Spiritual vessel, *Pray for us.*
Vessel of honor, *Pray for us.*
Singular vessel of devotion, *Pray for us.*
Mystical rose, *Pray for us.*
Tower of David, *Pray for us.*
Tower of ivory, *Pray for us.*
House of gold, *Pray for us.*
Ark of the covenant, *Pray for us.*
Gate of heaven, *Pray for us.*
Morning star, *Pray for us.*
Health of the sick, *Pray for us.*
Refuge of sinners, *Pray for us.*
Comforter of the afflicted, *Pray for us.*
Help of Christians, *Pray for us.*
Queen of angels, *Pray for us.*
Queen of patriarchs, *Pray for us.*
Queen of prophets, *Pray for us.*
Queen of apostles, *Pray for us.*
Queen of martyrs, *Pray for us.*
Queen of confessors, *Pray for us.*
Queen of virgins, *Pray for us.*
Queen of all saints, *Pray for us.*
Queen conceived without original sin, *Pray for us.*
Queen assumed into heaven, *Pray for us.*
Queen of the most holy Rosary, *Pray for us.*
Queen of peace, *Pray for us.*

Lamb of God, who takest away the sins, *Spare as, O Lord.*
Lamb of God, who takest away the sins , *Graciously hear us, O Lord.*
Lamb of God, Who takest away the sins, *Have mercy on us.*

Pray for us, O holy Mother of God. *That we may be made worthy of the promises of Christ.*

Let Us Pray: Pour forth, we beseech Thee, O Lord, Thy grace into our hearts; that we to whom the Incarnation of Christ Thy Son was made known by the message of an angel, may by His passion and cross be brought to the glory of His Resurrection; through the same Christ Our Lord. *Amen.*

May the divine assistance remain always with us. *Amen.*

And may the souls of the faithful departed, through the mercy of God, rest in peace. *Amen.*

Litany of the Holy Name of Jesus

Lord, have mercy on us,
Christ, have mercy on us.
Lord, have mercy on us.

Jesus, hear us. *Jesus, graciously hear us.*

God the Father of Heaven, *Have mercy on us.*
God the Son, Redeemer of the world, *Have mercy on us.*
God the Holy Ghost, *Have mercy on us.*
Holy Trinity, One God, *Have mercy on us.*
Jesus, Son of the living God, *Have mercy on us.*
Jesus, splendor of the Father, *Have mercy on us.*
Jesus, brightness of eternal light, *Have mercy on us.*
Jesus, King of glory, *Have mercy on us.*
Jesus, Sun of justice, *Have mercy on us.*
Jesus, Son of the Virgin Mary, *Have mercy on us.*
Jesus, most amiable, *Have mercy on us.*
Jesus, most admirable, *Have mercy on us.*
Jesus, mighty God, *Have mercy on us.*
Jesus, Father of the world to come, *Have mercy on us.*
Jesus, Angel of the great counsel, *Have mercy on us.*
Jesus, most powerful, *Have mercy on us.*
Jesus, most patient, *Have mercy on us.*
Jesus, most obedient, *Have mercy on us.*
Jesus, meek and humble of heart, *Have mercy on us.*
Jesus, Lover of chastity, *Have mercy on us.*
Jesus, Lover of us, *Have mercy on us.*
Jesus, God of peace, *Have mercy on us.*
Jesus, Author of life, *Have mercy on us.*
Jesus, Model of virtues, *Have mercy on us.*
Jesus, zealous for souls, *Have mercy on us.*
Jesus, our God, *Have mercy on us.*
Jesus, our Refuge, *Have mercy on us.*

Jesus, Father of the poor, *Have mercy on us.*
Jesus, Treasure of the faithful, *Have mercy on us.*
Jesus, Good Shepherd, *Have mercy on us.*
Jesus, true Light, *Have mercy on us.*
Jesus, eternal Wisdom, *Have mercy on us.*
Jesus, infinite Goodness, *Have mercy on us.*
Jesus, our Way and our Life, *Have mercy on us.*
Jesus, Joy of Angels, *Have mercy on us.*
Jesus, King of Patriarchs, *Have mercy on us.*
Jesus, Master of Apostles, *Have mercy on us.*
Jesus, Teacher of Evangelists, *Have mercy on us.*
Jesus, Strength of Martyrs, *Have mercy on us.*
Jesus, Light of Confessors, *Have mercy on us.*
Jesus, Purity of Virgins, *Have mercy on us.*
Jesus, Crown of all Saints, *Have mercy on us.*

Be merciful, *Spare us, O Jesus.*
Be merciful, *Graciously hear us, O Jesus.*

From all evil, *Jesus, deliver us.*
From all sin, *Jesus, deliver us.*
From Thy wrath, *Jesus, deliver us.*
From the snares of the devil, *Jesus, deliver us.*
From the spirit of fornication, *Jesus, deliver us.*
From everlasting death, *Jesus, deliver us.*
From the neglect of Thine inspirations, *Jesus, deliver us.*
Through the mystery of Thy holy Incarnation, *Jesus, deliver us.*
Through Thy Nativity, *Jesus, deliver us.*
Through Thine Infancy, *Jesus, deliver us.*
Through Thy most divine life, *Jesus, deliver us.*
Through Thy labors, *Jesus, deliver us.*
Through Thine Agony and Passion, *Jesus, deliver us.*
Through Thy Cross and dereliction, *Jesus, deliver us.*
Through Thy faintness and weariness, *Jesus, deliver us.*
Through Thy death and burial, *Jesus, deliver us.*

Through Thy Resurrection, *Jesus, deliver us.*
Through Thine Ascension, *Jesus, deliver us.*
Through Thine institution of the Most Holy Eucharist, *Jesus, deliver us.*
Through Thy joys, *Jesus, deliver us.*
Through Thy glory, *Jesus, deliver us.*

Lamb of God, Who takest away the sins of the world, *Spare us, O Jesus.*
Lamb of God, Who takest away the sins of the world, *Graciously hear us, O Jesus.*
Lamb of God, Who takest away the sins of the world, *Have mercy on us, O Jesus.*

Jesus, hear us. *Jesus, graciously hear us.*

Let Us Pray: O Lord Jesus Christ, Who hast said: "Ask and ye shall receive; seek, and ye shall find; knock, and it shall be opened unto you"; grant, we beseech Thee, to us who ask, the gift of Thy most divine love, that we may ever love Thee with all our heart, and in all our words and actions, and never cease from praising Thee.

Make us, O Lord, to have both a perpetual fear and love of Thy holy name, for Thou never failest to govern those whom Thou foundest upon the strength of Thy love, Who livest and reignest, world without end. *Amen.*

Consecration to Jesus Christ the Incarnate Wisdom through the Hands of Mary
(from "Love of the Eternal Wisdom" by
St. Louis-Marie Grignion de Montfort)

O Eternal and Incarnate Wisdom! O most loveable and adorable Jesus, true God and true man, only Son of the Eternal Father and of Mary Ever Virgin!

I adore You profoundly in the bosom and the splendors of Your Father from all eternity, and in the virginal womb of Mary, Your worthy Mother, in the time of Your Incarnation.

I give You thanks that You emptied Yourself, in taking the form of a slave, to rescue me from the cruel slavery of the Devil; I praise and glorify You for Your having desired to place Yourself in submission to Mary, Your Holy Mother, in all things, in order to make me, through her, Your faithful slave.

But alas! Ungrateful and unfaithful as I am, I have not kept the vows and promises which I solemnly made at my Baptism: I have not at all fulfilled my obligations; I do not merit to be called Your child or Your slave, and since there is nothing in me which merits anything but Your rejection and Your anger, I dare not approach any more on my own Your holy and august Majesty.

This is why I have recourse to the intercession and mercy of Your Most Holy Mother, whom You have given me as Mediatrix before You, and it is by this means that I hope to obtain from You contrition and pardon for my sins, and to acquire and preserve Wisdom.

Hail, O Immaculate Mary, living tabernacle of the Divinity, where the Eternal Hidden Wisdom desires to be adored by angels and men;

Hail, O Queen of Heaven and Earth, to whose rule everything that is below God is in submission;

Hail, O sure refuge of sinners, whose mercy extends to everyone;

Fulfill my longings for the Divine Wisdom, and receive for this purpose the vows and the offerings I present to you in my lowliness.

I, _____, an unfaithful sinner, renew and ratify today, through your hands, the vows of my Baptism:

I renounce forever Satan, his pomps and his works, and I give myself entirely to Jesus Christ, the Incarnate Wisdom, in order to carry my cross the rest of the days of my life, and to be more faithful than I have ever been before.

I choose you today, in the presence of the entire celestial court, as my Mother and my Mistress. I surrender to you and consecrate to you, as your slave, my body and soul, my interior and exterior possessions, and even the value of my good works past, present and future, leaving you the entire and complete right to dispose of me and all that belongs to me, without exception, according to your good pleasure, to the greater glory of God, for all time and eternity.

Receive, O Kind Virgin, this little offering of my slavery, in honor of the submission the Eternal Wisdom desired to have to your motherhood, in homage to the power that you both have over this little worm and wretched sinner, and in thanksgiving for the privileges with which the Holy Trinity has favored you.

I affirm my desire henceforth, as your true slave, to seek your honor and to obey you in everything.

O Admirable Mother, present me as an eternal slave to your dear Son, in order that, having accomplished my redemption through you, He might now receive me through you.

O Mother of Mercy, give me the grace to obtain the True Wisdom of God, and to this purpose let me be counted among those who love you, who are taught by you, who are nourished and protected by you, as your children and as your slaves.

O Faithful Virgin! Render me in everything such a perfect disciple, imitator and slave of the Incarnate Wisdom, Jesus Christ your Son, that I might reach, through your intercession, and following your example, the fullness of His age on Earth and of His glory in Heaven.

Amen.

CPSIA information can be obtained at www.ICGtesting.com
Printed in the USA
LVOW061626180612

286633LV00001B/225/A